# SEA OTTERS

# SEA OTTERS

## A Natural History and Guide

Roy Nickerson
Photography by Richard Bucich
Epilogue by Margaret Owings,
Founder and President, Friends of the Sea Otter

CHRONICLE BOOKS • SAN FRANCISCO

By the same author:

*Brother Whale*
*Hawaii: The Volcano State*
*Lahaina—Royal Capital of Hawaii*
*Robert Louis Stevenson in California*
*The Friendly Whales*

Printed in Hong Kong.

Library of Congress Cataloging-in-Publication Data

Nickerson, Roy.
   Sea otters: a natural history and guide / Roy Nickerson; photography by Richard Bucich.— [2nd ed.]
     p.    cm.
  Bibliography: p.
  Includes index.
  ISBN 0-87701-567-8 (pbk.)
  1. Sea otter.    I. Title.
  QL737.C25N53   1989          88-25737
  599.74'447—dc19            CIP

Editing: Deborah Stone
Book and cover design: Julie Noyes
Composition: TBH/Typecast, Inc., Cotati, CA

10  9  8  7  6  5  4  3  2  1

Chronicle Books
275 Fifth Street
San Francisco, California
94103

# Contents

*How can you resist a sea otter smile?*

# Introduction

Since the first edition of this book appeared in 1984, a number of good things — or at least encouraging things — have happened in the world of the California sea otter. Specifically, the state of California has firmed up laws banning the use of gill nets in certain offshore areas where sea otters as well as other marine mammals and birds were being trapped and drowned; the courts no longer treat Fish & Game laws as nuisances that serve only to clog court calendars; translocation of a reserve breeding population of sea otters has gotten under way; and the sea otter population at long last appears to show signs of renewed growth.

Over a recent ten-year period, some 100 sea otters have drowned each year after becoming entangled in fishermen's gill nets and trammel nets. (Gill nets trap fish when they attempt to escape through the mesh; trammel nets have three walls of webbing to accomplish the same purpose.) Large numbers of harbor porpoises and diving birds also fall victim to the nets; in less than ten years of gill netting, murre colonies on the Farallon Islands, just out the Golden Gate from San Francisco, have declined in population from 30,000 nesting pairs to about 7,000 nesting pairs.

The use of gill nets and trammel nets is now restricted within the 225-mile-long California sea otter range. Current state law prohibits their use altogether from Waddell Creek, just south of Point Año Nuevo (near Santa Cruz), to Point Sal, south of Morro Bay, in fifteen fathoms or less of water. There is an additional restriction to twenty fathoms from Point Sur to Pfeiffer Point — the historic "cradle" where the southern sea otter was preserved, virtually unseen by man, during the years when the species was thought to have been wiped out — and also in twenty fathoms from Cape San Martin to Pico Creek. Completely closed to these nets is the portion of Monterey Bay south of a line from the Monterey Beach Hotel (near the Monterey-Seaside border) to Point Pinos. The otters increasingly visible around Monterey Harbor and off Cannery Row are thus protected from the nets.

These laws have been enacted largely due to the urging of Friends of the Sea Otter, which now feels the limit should be extended to twenty fathoms throughout the range. Other concerned organizations have worked successfully for limits on the use of these nets north of the southern sea otter range in order to protect sea birds and other marine mammals.

One instance of the stronger enforcement of Fish & Game laws occurred as this is being written. A resident of Salinas, California, was sentenced to serve six months in the county jail and to pay fines and penalties totaling $1,900 for possessing a dead sea otter. He had attempted, unsuccessfully, to skin it. Furthermore, the woman who allowed the otter to be transported in her car was fined $1,000.

Also during this period, charges are pending against fishermen who hauled in three sea otters that drowned in the gill nets they had set illegally inside the twenty-fathom closure area off the Big Sur coast; both state and federal wildlife officials witnessed the act. In addition, researchers working at Cayucos, just north of Morro Bay, California, observed fishermen shooting sea otters. These biologists notified Coast Guard officials, who intercepted the suspects' skiff, recovered the body of a sea otter that had died of gunshot wounds, and had the witnesses identify the gunmen. Three were charged.

As a newspaper reporter, I remember years ago interviewing a game warden who expressed exasperation because the courts were so busy with what they considered "serious criminal matters," they would give "little notice to Fish & Game violations." Now, thanks to a number of conservation groups, including Friends of the Sea Otter in Carmel, jurists realize the importance and the urgency of laws enacted to protect the ecosystem, of which mankind is only one of many indispensable links.

During this time a sense of urgency was also added to the proposal to translocate sea otters, as more ships continued to either founder, drift dangerously close to shore during power losses, or even sink and start to ooze oil to the surface. In the event of a leak or spill, oil often drifts from the sea lanes and offshore oil drilling rigs toward the coast, posing a danger to sea otters. For this reason, Friends of the Sea Otter successfully urged the establishment of a "reserve breeding colony" of otters on San Nicolas Island. One of the California Channel Islands, San Nicolas is farthest from shore, to the west of the shipping lanes.

Translocation from established colonies near shore started with the capture of several sea otters August 24, 1987. They were examined by a veterinarian at the Monterey Bay Aquarium, monitored for two days to minimize stress, then flown to San Nicolas and released after being acclimated in floating pens. Sixty animals were sent before a pause was ordered to assess the progress of the operation. During the ensuing months, three otters were found to have died, apparently of stress. Three more died of other causes, including drowning from entanglement in either gill nets or lobster traps. Two were found dead off the Southern California mainland, one shot.

Amazingly, by the spring of 1988, nine additional "missing" otters had turned up back off the Big Sur coast where they had been captured. So strong was the homing instinct of these older otters that they swam 150 miles back to where they came from. Their actions provided a valuable addition to our knowledge of sea otters, and young otters, less set in their ways, will be used in future moves.

As Friends of the Sea Otter's executive secretary Carol Fulton has stated, "We never thought translocation would be a 'quick fix,' and realized that it would probably take many years before the success or failure of the breeding colony would be known. . . . To put the painful loss of these animals in perspective, however, we must remember that at least six otters were shot in Monterey Bay alone last year. . . . For over a decade we were losing roughly 100 otters a year in fishing nets . . . and should a major oil spill occur, we could lose hundreds and hundreds of otters."

Until nineteenth-century trappers decimated their numbers, sea otters numbered between 16,000 and 20,000 in California alone. Today this population is estimated at approximately 1,700. So while much that I have described is encouraging news, it must also be remembered that the present population is a fraction of that which existed along the Golden Coast before man nearly wiped it out. Ironically, the present population exists almost entirely thanks to man's efforts in this more enlightened age.

Roy Nickerson
Carmel, 1989

#  The Smallest of Them All

Along the thousands of miles of the northern Pacific Coast, from Mexico to the former realm of the Russian tsars, there is one place that holds a special magic for me above all others. It consists of about 1,300 acres—some 450 acres of land adjacent to 750 acres under water, where marine mammals and scuba divers play, plus 150 acres across the Coastal Highway, where a unique grove of trees is preserved.

Located about four miles south of Carmel, California, this magic place is often swept by a chill wind, and the surf beats itself into a salty frenzy against an amazing collection of boulders, pinnacles and cliffs. At one time the site had been staked out with neat rows of twine to show how it could be subdivided into a busy little community of streets and houses.

Fortunately, that plan fell through and in the late 1920s the Save-the-Redwoods League, as well as some concerned private citizens, decided the unique beauty of this place should be preserved, possibly under the stewardship of the State of California. A study was commissioned which eventually won the State's interest. In 1933 California took over the initial portion of what has become known today as Point Lobos State Reserve.

Magic is different things to different people. Point Lobos is magic to me because through the years I have been able to sit at the edges of its coves and I have been treated to what I consider to be the Greatest Show on Earth.

The show goes on all year round and reaches its height during the months of winter and early spring. Off the coast a magnificent parade of gray whales heads south to the lagoons of Baja California where their young will be born in warm waters; several months later, they head back to the rich, cold waters of Alaska to feed.

Overhead whirls a friendly mixture of kittiwakes, Western and Bonaparte's gulls, cormorants and guillemots. Brown pelicans share the air space in increasing numbers. The gulls aren't above begging, and they'll approach a picnic table with only a minimum of caution. The cormorants fly in formation low over the water looking for schools of fish. Early in the spring they go individually to the kelp beds and bring back strands to the rocks to prepare their nests. One of nature's mysteries is how as awkward-looking a bird as a pelican can appear so graceful as it flies, follow-the-leader fashion, around the ends of Point Lobos looking for fishy fare.

Stage center—in the midst of spouting and breaching whales and swooping and searching birds—close to shore, in slowly but blessedly increasing numbers, are the stars of the show: the sea otters. All of this activity takes place within sight of a single glance.

For a long time the Pacific shores were barren of sea otters. Today off the central California coast they are making a precarious and limited comeback, in part thanks to human help. The phrase "barren of sea otters" is only a slight exaggeration. A small raft did cling to life off an isolated spot of the Big Sur coast. A select few knew about it and, to their credit, over the years kept their mouths shut. This allowed the otters to stabilize their numbers and start to increase. In 1938 a Monterey photographer braved the treacherous cliff and got close enough with his camera to photograph the group and display it to the world.

That photo caused both joy and consternation. Nature lovers and scientists were overjoyed to see that the sea otter had survived the brutal onslaught of fur traders in its southern range. There was the comforting fact that a series of treaties, laws and proclamations dating from 1911 protected the sea otters from hunters. Some wondered how the secret had been kept for so long. And a few worried that the discovery would bring out mindless poachers with only profit in view.

To the joy of most who delight in watching the habits and antics of the smallest of the world's marine mammals—and admittedly to the dismay of a few who would rather get rich off the abalone and clam market—*Enhydra lutris* is still with us and has cautiously extended its range.

At one time the sea otters happily inhabited the warm waters of southern California and upper Baja California, about as far south as Morro Hermoso and San Benito Island, which are located halfway down that Mexican peninsula. The fur traders of the eighteenth century considered them to be furry little gold nuggets and soon reduced them to the point where it was hardly worth mounting an expedition to go after them. Isolated groups rafting together, sometimes only a single sea otter or one accompanied by a family member, managed to survive in hidden pockets along the coast. (A *raft* tends to be composed of separate gender groupings of sea otters, or females with their baby, except during mating.) The appetite of the hunter for wealth was so voracious, and his mind so devoid of the consequences of wiping out the source of his wealth, that he would track down even a single sea otter.

Often the best information we have about the survival of the sea otters comes from the very people who were out to exterminate them—the hunters. Their accounts tell us that small and innocent numbers of sea otters managed to endure, some of which were ancestors of the historic raft photographed off Big Sur in 1938. The survivors were few and were widely spread out, where before the population had not been broken up into such isolated groupings.

In the University of California's authoritative *Fur-Bearing Mammals of California*, published in 1937, the authors recorded:

*Writing about sea otters 30 years ago, Stephens (1906, p. 233) considered them to be rare everywhere at that time. According to him, a few were still living about the islands off the coast of Lower and southern California. They "frequent kelp beds among rocky islets," he said, "where they feed on mussels, clams, sea urchins and other mollusks, fish and kelp. They are excessively shy, and their senses are acute; hence they are very difficult to obtain. The single young are brought forth at any season, the intervals apparently being more than a year. The young are said to suckle more than a year."*

*In 1918 Mr. W. J. Evans, who lived near San Carpoforo Creek in San Luis Obispo County, told one of us [Joseph Grinnell, one of the three authors of the study] that in several previous winters he had hunted sea otter along the coast north from that locality to Point Sur. Seven men in three open boats made up a "crew," and the animals were to be shot about the rocky headlands and kelp beds only in calm weather. Three was the largest number ever taken in one trip. The highest price received for one skin, the best one, was $250. As many as forty otters were seen in one day. According to Mr. Evans, four otters were seen and "shot at" near Punta Gorda two or three years before 1918.*

*In 1912 Mr. E. C. Dearborn of Sacramento said (Taylor, MS) that he had been a member of an expedition in 1890 which took sea otters off Pigeon Point, not far south of San Francisco, and near San Miguel Island off the coast of southern California. Dearborn had seen a sea otter in a shallow place near the wave-washed shore, but he had never seen one on land.*

*Two of the late records of the occurrence of sea otters on the California coast were printed in one issue of* California Fish and Game. *P. H. Oyer (1917, p. 88) reported: "Two sea otters were seen basking in the sun in the kelp beds off Del Monte between Seaside and Del Monte wharf on October 22, 1916. They were apparently an old and a young one, and the theory is that the old one came back to look for one of her young which was caught in a sea-bass net last year." George Farnsworth (1917, p. 90) wrote: "On March 18, 1916, 31 sea otters, two being young ones, were seen to the south of Catalina Island."*

Sea otters are still drowning in fishermen's nets today, and that couple described as "basking in the kelp beds off Del Monte" has become a raft of up to a dozen. Today the Monterey harbor tour boats take passengers to roughly the same location to view sea otters: about halfway between Municipal Wharf No. 2 and Del Monte Beach as it hits Seaside. After that, the tour boats head for Cannery Row, where more sea otters may often be seen in the kelp beds off Monterey Bay Aquarium.

Pigeon Point is just to the north of the present northern limit of the southern sea otter. A note to the *Otter Raft*, the publication of Friends of the Sea Otter, confirms the existence of a baby sea otter and its mother at the beginning of 1979, along with a male which may or may not be the father, at Santa Cruz Point (locally called Lighthouse Point). Pigeon Point is 26 miles up the coast from this sighting.

The Piedras Blancas Lighthouse at San Simeon, where the U.S. Fish and Wildlife Service maintains a field station for observation and research, roughly marks the present southern limit of the sea otters. The lighthouse is located in typical sea otter country—rocky shoreline with cliffs and sheltered inlets, offshore kelp beds and an abundance of food. The otters' southern range ends about 25 miles south of this lighthouse at Morro Bay and Pismo Beach—much to the dismay of those humans who would rather harvest the Pismo clams for themselves.

According to a paper published in 1978 by the Southern California Academy of Sciences, isolated sea otter sightings have been reported in the Channel Islands off Santa Barbara in recent years as well as off Santa Monica Bay. In 1979 there was one sighting inside Los Angeles Harbor and another further to the south off Point Loma at San Diego.

These isolated sightings have been so rare that marine biologists do not consider them sufficient to say that the sea otter has extended its range that far south. The larger rafts of otters appear to stop at Morro Bay. While these otters are within their historic range, the sightings are amazing because the otters—along with some other sea dwellers—seem to do poorly in areas like Los Angeles and San Diego, where large human populations have been built up and where the accompanying pollution extends out to sea.

Sea otters don't appear to observe any particular mating season but get together just about any time they feel like it, producing an offspring no more than once a year, usually between December and March. Like some other marine mammals, the sea otter is capable of delayed implantation, that is, delaying the start of the fertilization, and thus the growth, of the embryo. I have been unable to find any scientific discussion as to why the sea otters do this, but I'm sure they have their reasons! I have visited the elephant seals at Año Nuevo (north of Santa Cruz), where I learned that they are among the other marine mammals that delay the start of the embryo's development. University of California docents acting as guides there said this was so the baby could be born on land, for this brief winter visit is the only time of year the elephant seals haul out.

For the most part, sea otters are born at sea amidst the kelp beds. A clump of kelp has often been referred to romantically in writing as the sea otters' cradle. Sea otters do not migrate. Once they 've established a territory, most tend to stay there.

The authors of the Southern California Academy of Sciences bulletin (77[3], 1978) sadly noted:

*If there were, indeed, sea otters at Santa Catalina Island as late as 1917, it may safely be assumed that this relict aggregate was harassed into extinction, as enforcement in the insular area was difficult at that time. Kenyon (1969) reported that a remnant population at San Benito Island, Baja California, was hunted to extinction in 1919, and that a small population at Queen Charlotte Island, British Columbia, was extirpated by hunters in 1920. Thus the remnant population at Point Sur, California was very probably the only viable aggregation that survived beyond 1920 south of Prince William Sound, Alaska. No wanderers were reported in Baja California or California outside Monterey County from 1917 to 1940.*

It is little wonder then, that Point Lobos Superintendent Jim Whitehead permitted himself a slightly emotional log entry on Feb. 20, 1954:

*Eureka! and Huzzah! This is a great and momentous day in the modern history of Point Lobos Reserve. While on patrol to Gibson Beach I saw a Sea Otter playing off Mr. Kellogg's property (south end of Gibson Beach) at approximately 3:30 P.M. There were at least one, maybe two, coming into the Reserve itself.*

*A thrilling event to me, and with great possibilities for the Reserve. For with the animals that close and the food supply available here, we could within a reasonable amount of time, have a flourishing colony here in the Reserve.*

I don't know what Mr. Whitehead would have considered "a flourishing colony," but visitors to Point Lobos today can usually count on seeing sea otters. In the winter-spring period of 1982–83, I thought perhaps the otters were hiding in the coves to get away from the terrible storms at sea that accompanied the El Niño phenomenon. I noticed them in increased numbers in the very same coves the winter and spring later. On calm days several can be seen off Gibson Beach, which is the southern boundary of the Reserve.

In one recent visit I saw a lone sea otter happily eating something as he floated on his back in the Caribbean blue-green translucence of China Cove, which is the next cove north from Gibson Beach and Bird Rock. All the way around Point Lobos to Whalers Cove, there were five of them leapfrogging among themselves, occasionally disappearing beneath the surface, then returning with some morsel. Northward again—bypassing the next little cove where I have seen them on other visits—to the Reserve's northernmost cove off Moss Beach and the great meadow that used to be the late Admiral Hudson's back yard (this part of the Reserve was once Hudson property). In this cove there were four more sea otters. A total of 10 otters on one visit is a very remarkable sighting indeed!

This last group of four exhibited typical sea otter behavior. Three of them were "strapped" seatbelt-like atop a small bed of kelp where they gently swayed back and forth with the water's surge, apparently snoozing, secure in the knowledge that they could not be hurled out of their natural cradle by a sudden wave.

The fourth one, much closer to shore, kept diving and reappearing with what appeared to be some sort of a mollusc. He was on his back. He had a rather flat stone on his tummy which he always carried down with him, probably secured in the pouchlike fold of skin between his forearm and his chest. When he returned to the surface, he had the stone with him, at the same time clutching his newfound tidbit in his paws. Floating on his back again, he took the morsel and beat it furiously against the rock resting on his stomach. When it broke open, he quickly slurped out his lunch.

Once again, with the precision of an Olympic swimmer, he flipped over onto his stomach, arched his back and disappeared with the rock beneath the water in search of his next snack.

*Following page: Otters use their handlike forepaws to fluff their fur. Their hind legs are paddlelike flippers.* ▶

*This resting sea otter does not look happy at being disturbed.*

*A group of sea otters bob among seaweed.*

*This sea otter pokes his head through a pile of kelp.*

*Following page: His whiskers give this otter a worried look.* ▶

*Sea otters sleep on their backs — and in a water bed..*

*A resting sea otter reclines in kelp-strewn water.*

# All in the Family

The Russians called them *bobri morski*, or sea beavers, because their early hunters ignored the shapes of the tails and examined only the richness of the pelts. Scientists have described three different subspecies of sea otter, mostly based on geographical location. They also found minor differences in skull size and other physical characteristics, but these variations occurred in different geographical areas and could be attributed to a number of things.

While there is continuing scientific debate over how many subspecies of sea otter there are, there is one, and only one, species of sea otter: *Enhydra lutris*. This scientific name comes from some amazingly uncomplicated thinking: *en hydra* is Greek for "in the water," and *lutris* is the Latin word for "otter."

Karl W. Kenyon, retired wildlife biologist for the federal Fish and Wildlife Service, explains the early attempt at creating three subspecies of sea otter in his definitive work, *The Sea Otter in the Eastern Pacific Ocean*. Researchers have classified the otters that live in the northern reaches of their range as *Enhydra lutris lutris*, the otters from the Canadian border south to Baja California as *Enhydra lutris nereis*, and those in Siberian waters as *Enhydra lutris gracilis*.

However, Kenyon says in his book: "After superficial examination of several hundred sea otters taken at Amchitka Island . . . and after observing the variation in color and body size among animals of this local population, I agree with Scheffer and Wilke (1950). They studied specimens from California and the Aleutian Islands and reviewed the basis for establishing a racial division. They concluded that 'Neither on a basis of demonstrable variation nor on the grounds of geographical isolation is there

support for a southern subspecies of the sea otter.'"

A thorough examination of whether there are three subspecies or not has no place in a book for laypersons such as this. Recent research has revived arguments for insisting that there are three subspecies. As an amateur naturalist, I feel the important thing is to recognize that there are two populations: the northern, off Alaskan and Soviet shores, and the southern, off California.

The sea otter belongs to the overall family known as *Mustelidae*. These mammals bear and nurse living young, just like the great whales and humans. They are meat eaters and as members of the *Mustelidae* family they are supposed to be musk bearers. The sea otter is the one member of the family that does not have anal scent glands. One relative bearing these glands is the skunk: If it seems strange that the cuddly sea otter and the skunk should be relatives, remember that China's giant panda is in the same family as America's raccoon!

Sea otters are believed to have come into being more than a million years ago in southern Asia. They migrated northward, took to the sea, and remained there. They evolved in the Pleistocene epoch, or the Ice Age, when human beings first reached Europe and North America and when large animals such as mammoths roamed the earth. There are fossilized remains to prove that the diminutive sea otter has changed little from this time. Otters are related to the ferret, the badger, the wolverine, the marten, the mink—including the extinct sea mink— and, of course, the river otter. The weasel—with the uncomplimentary images the term conjures up—is a member of the same family.

The sea otter has been the subject of a number of articles and books. One of the latest is *The Amazing Sea Otter* by Victor B. Scheffer, another retired wildlife biologist of the Fish and Wildlife Service and a former co-worker with Kenyon. After his retirement, Scheffer wrote several books on different marine mammals and created much interest in them.

More than anyone else, the late Gavin Maxwell must be credited with bringing the otter family to the world's attention. He wrote his book, *Ring of Bright Water*, in 1959 and by the time the first American edition came out less than two years later, Edal and Mijbil were almost household words. These were the names of two of the river otters he brought from the Mideast to London and from there to his isolated Highland home.

A fire destroyed the cottage in the late 1960s as well as panic-striken Edal. Another otter, Teko, survived the blaze and eventually took up a new home with Maxwell in another isolated part of Scotland, the small lighthouse island of Kyleakin, at Skye. Here Maxwell hoped to build a nature retreat not only for his pet otters but for the animals and birds native to Scotland. The dream ended unrealized with his death of lung cancer in 1969. His books on nature, along with a subsequent book by an associate of his—*The White Island*, by John Lister-Kaye—remain to charm people who delight in otters. For the most part, public interest in these animals has been coupled with an interest in their conservation. People, anxious to see sea otters even when they are not there, have reported vast herds of them bobbing in the surf along the California coast. (Nowadays, a sighting of a half-dozen sea otters is a highly successful event.) What they have sighted is an offshore bed of kelp—agreed, a likely place for sea otters. The bobbing "otter heads" are the bulbs at the end of the strands of kelp that keep them stretched from the ocean floor to the water's surface.

In the American Northwest, there is also occasional confusion between river otters and sea otters. Alice Seed, in her paper on sea otters published in 1972 by Pacific Search, wrote:

*We often receive reports from residents or visitors in Washington's San Juan Islands that they have seen sea otters. After investigating many of these, we found that in every case the reports concerned river otters, which are abundant in salt water among the San Juans and other islands north to Alaska. The differences between the two species are easily observed. The sea otter always eats while floating high on its back in the water. It never goes out onto the rocks to eat as the river otter frequently does. Also, the river otter has a relatively long tail (about one-half its body length), heavily thickened at its base, while the sea otter has a relatively short (about one-third its body length), flattened tail. It seems unlikely that sea otters ever frequented the area of the San Juan Islands. In early times, explorers recorded that they could not get sea otter skins from natives of the inland waters but had to get them from Nootka Sound and other areas of the outer coast.*

There are other differences between river and sea otters. The river otter is a smaller animal: Males rarely weigh more than 35 pounds, while the male sea otter averages 60 pounds. The front and back feet of the river otter are webbed while in the sea otter only the back feet are webbed. The sea otter's front feet are more like "hands" to be used for grasping. These front paws are so unique, in fact, that the sea otter is the only marine mammal that catches fish with its "hands" instead of its teeth. The only continent where river otters are not found is Australia, while the sea otter has an extremely limited range.

River otters eat fish and shellfish, as do sea otters; occasionally they eat small birds, mammals such as muskrats, frogs and even insects. The sea otter loves shellfish, crabs, sea urchins and sometimes small fish. Compared with their salt water relatives, river otters have something of a mating season, with babies usually born between February and June in nests hollowed out of the earth along the banks of rivers and lakes. Sea otters are almost always born at sea, with the kelp beds their cradle. Both have about the same gestation period (two months) but the sea otter can delay the start of actual implantation of the semen for three, four or even five months. Sea otter pups can be born seven months and more after mating takes place.

Man seems to be the most dangerous enemy for both the river and the sea otter. There have been isolated reports of bald eagles snatching up a baby sea otter and scattered reports that great white sharks have attacked them. Shark attacks seem to be accidental, caused by ignorance as to what they are. Dead sea otters with shark teeth in them have been found, but I have been unable to locate a recording of sea otter remains found in a shark's stomach.

Sea otters are known to swim among the orcas, or killer whales, in northern waters but apparently they do not bother each other. I have reports of sea otters being frightened or scattered by a pod of killer whales, but these accounts seem to have been written out of a common ignorance of the orca's reputation as a killer. (They are called killer whales only because they will prey on other whales when hungry, not because they are dangerous to man—or sea otters!)

Perhaps the oddest difference between river and sea otter, at least to an amateur naturalist such as myself, is the fact that the river otter has a thick layer of fat under its skin and fur, and the sea otter does not. It would seem reasonable to assume that the sea otter is able to spend most of its life in the chill water of the North Pacific because it is insulated by a protective layer of blubber. This is not so. The sea otter's unique and beautiful fur coat traps air to keep it warm, and its voracious appetite keeps the calories burning. The sea otter needs up to 20 pounds of fresh food every day, about one-quarter its body weight. It appears to digest and pass its food in as little as three hours.

Because it lacks the blubber that keeps many other marine mammals warm, the sea otter is "entirely dependent for warmth on an insulating blanket of air trapped among its tightly packed fur fibers," Kenyon writes. "These fibers may number approximately 800 million hairs . . . Because the otter's survival depends on the insulation of its fur coat, its molt is diffuse, taking place during the entire year. Although molt is continuous, more fur fibers are shed in midsummer than in midwinter. The pelage color varies from nearly black to various shades of brown. Light or blond-colored animals are rare. Although most sea otter pelts look quite similar, it is difficult to match exactly even three or four skins out of 100 (J. S. Vania personal communication). Guard hairs vary in color with individuals, from white to black."

Sometimes older sea otters actually turn silvery or white around the head, just as humans do.

Sea otters are extremely clean; to be otherwise can mean death. Any dirt or interference in the cleanliness of their coat—or pelage, as the biologists say when referring to it—can be fatal. Attempts to hold sea otters captive, or translocate them in the wild in order to widen their range or give them a chance at survival, have shown the importance of grooming; sea otters kept in cages for only a few hours before being released again into water have died because their coats became dirty.

Grooming takes up a considerable part of a sea otter's day. They go at it with great energy before they take their rest periods. While resting, floating leisurely on their backs, they will groom themselves, almost as if by reflex, before dozing off. A mother grooms her baby whenever she isn't grooming herself or gathering food; the pup learns the importance of grooming almost before it learns the need for food!

*Following page: Otters strap themselves in with kelp much like a human straps on a seat belt—except in this case, the kelp keeps an otter from drifting away.* ▶

*This sea otter looks mildly surprised to see a foot emerging from the water.*

*◄ Previous page: Constant grooming is necessary for sea otters—the cold water must never touch their skin.*

*I can still touch my toes.*

# The Fur West

"The most valuable fur-bearing animals inhabiting the waters of the North-western Coast of North America are the Sea Otters."

That opening sentence in his chapter on sea otters, found in Capt. Charles M. Scammon's remarkable book, *The Marine Mammals of the Northwestern Coast of North America,* captures more than 200 years of human—and inhuman—history in a nutshell.

The American sea captain wrote his book in 1874. It continues to fascinate anyone interested in sea otters and their history. Capt. Scammon was born in Maine in 1825 and headed for California 25 years later. He undertook voyages from the Galapagos to Alaska in search of oil-yielding marine mammals ranging from elephant seals to the great whales. He is the one who discovered the secret of the gray whales: They disappeared from the sea lanes in winter because they entered one of the several lagoons on the Pacific coast of Baja California. Today the lagoon Mexicans label Ojo de Liebre is known to most of us as Scammon's Lagoon.

When the Civil War broke out, Scammon entered what was then the U.S. Revenue Service—now known as the U.S. Coast Guard—as a captain. He remained with the Service until he retired in the mid-1890s, having proved himself both an able master mariner and a remarkable amateur zoologist. He died in 1911.

His book was privately printed and few copies of the original edition remain. Today we are indebted to Dover Publications of New York for making a facsimile edition, with a modern introduction by Dr. Scheffer, available to the public. Most of Scammon's observations are still valid. More to the point, the book provides fascinating eyewitness accounts of nineteenth century sailing and hunting, and therefore a vivid picture of what has happened to so many marine mammals.

Here is the rest of Capt. Scammon's opening description of the sea otter; keep in mind he was writing more than a century ago when he describes the "existing population":

*They are found as far south as twenty-eight degrees north latitude, and their northern limits include the Aleutian Islands. Although never migrating to the southern hemisphere, these peculiar amphibious animals are found around the isolated points of southern Kamchatka and even to the western Kuriles, a chain of islands that separates the Okhotsk Sea from the north-eastern Pacific. The length of the full-grown animal may average five feet, including the tail, which is about ten inches. The head resembles that of the Fur Seal. The eyes of the Sea Otter are full, black, and piercing, and exhibit much intelligence. The color of the female, when "in season," is quite black; at other periods, it is a dark brown. The males are usually of the same shade, although, in some instances, they are of a jet, shining black, like their mates. The fur is of a much lighter shade inside than upon the surface, and, extending over all, are scattering, long, glistening hairs, which add much to the richness and beauty of the pelage. Some individuals, about the nose and eyes, are of a light brown or dingy white. The ears are less than an inch in length, quite pointed, standing nearly erect, and are covered with short hair. Occasionally, the young are of a deep brown, with the ends of the longest hairs tipped with white, and, about the nose and eyes, of a cream color.*

*The hind feet, or flippers, of the animal are webbed, much like the seal's. It fore legs are short, the fore paws resembling those of a cat, being furnished with five sharp claws, as are the posterior flippers.*

The sea otter's brush with extinction started in the early eighteenth century when the Chinese mandarins, or nobles, first were introduced to this richest of pelts by Russian hunters. They paid fabulous prices to have robes made out of them. When the Russians discovered the sea otter, the fur also soon became the envy of St. Petersburg, and later Paris. Capt. James Cook of the Royal Navy found sea otters when he was searching for a northwest passage. Through him, not only did London learn of sea otter fur but so did the Boston sea captains. What otters the Russians didn't locate, the Yankee seamen and fur trappers did.

Strictly speaking, the sea otters' troubles can be traced back to Tsar Ivan the Terrible. The expeditions he sent out across the Asian vastness brought the Russians to Siberia. Ivan IV died in 1560, never knowing about the eastern Pacific discoveries. One of his successors, however, Peter I (the Great), became the first Russian emperor to decide that Russia should emerge from the introversion that had characterized his nation up until then. He commissioned the Danish sea captain Vitus Jonassen Bering to go to the eastern shores of the Motherland. Bering was to build ships, make expeditions to discover if Siberia were connected with the North American mainland, and establish a Russian presence in the outside world.

Peter the Great gave Bering his commission in 1724 but was denied enjoyment of the fruits of his imagination. He died in 1725; Bering did not return until three years later. Because the results of his first expedition were not appreci-

ated, Bering sought a second expedition. This was granted by the new monarch, the Empress Anne. He left St. Petersburg in 1733 with a large company, some 600 men, but without the backup he really needed to mount such an ambitious undertaking. Two ships were used. Aboard the vessel captained by Bering himself was the German zoologist, George Steller, who made the first scientific observations and descriptions of the marine mammals of the North Pacific, and whose name is preserved in such designations as Steller's Sea Lion.

In November 1741 Bering's ship, the *St. Peter*, crashed on the shores of an island called Bering Island, off Kamchatka, after taking a terrific beating in storms and being lost in fog. Bering subsequently died. He survived just long enough to catch his first glimpse of the little animal we now call the sea otter. The beasts had never seen man before and had no reason to fear them. They went up to the haggard Russians like a group of kittens seeking lunch. As they rubbed their noses joyously against the legs of the hungry sailors, they were bludgeoned to death, then skinned and eaten.

The survivors of the shipwreck finally returned home, gaunt with scurvy but clothed in furs that excited Chinese mandarin and Russian aristocrat alike. Wealthy Russian merchants founded fur trading companies and those with the means to mount their own expeditions speedily did so. Among the sea captains retained was Gerassim Pribilof, whose name is familiar to us today because he left his name on the Alaskan fur seal islands.

Another, Grigor Shelekhov, whose name is not so well known, really got the ball rolling. He decided that if the reigning monarch, Empress Catherine the Great—who adopted the French *laissez faire* approach to government intervention in business affairs—would not finance and protect a mercantile expedition, then he would privately. In 1783 he had three ships built to sail to the sea otter islands. He and his wife Natalya sailed aboard one of them, the *Three Saints*, skippered by Capt. Stepan Izmailov. This began a reign of terror for both the sea otters, which quickly learned to be wary of man, and the Aleuts and other native people of what is now Alaska.

The Russians went after sea otters with such determination that entire herds were wiped out. Catherine the Great's death brought about the demise of the *laissez faire* doctrine and a tax for the tsar of one-tenth of the value of the shipments was imposed. In the eastern extremes of Russia, the scattered trading companies united under the collective umbrella of the Russian-American Fur Company.

Shelekhov persuaded the shrewd merchant Alexander Andreevich Baranov to take charge of the new arrangement. For more than three decades, Baranov reigned as the first governor of Russian America, ultimately setting up headquarters in New Archangel, now known as Sitka.

Baranov ran his company smoothly and firmly, so much so that he has come down in history known variously as "the little tzar" and the Lord of Alaska. He explored a variety of plans to extend the Russian empire and briefly toyed with the idea of adding the Hawaiian Islands to the tsar's crown. Primarily, Baranov set himself to bringing order out of the chaos of the early *laissez faire* days, which saw the freelance fur hunters, known as the *promyschleniki,* nearly decimate the sea otter population.

It was evident that a more organized method of hunting was necessary, as was a more organized manner of consolidating mammal pelt shipments, protecting them and maintaining the prices. It was a man of more noble birth who brought some reason to the old Russian hunting ways. Shelekhov had married off one of his daughters to a shareholder in the new company, Count Nicolai Petrovich De Rezanov. The Count was a stockholder in the company, as were members of the Imperial Family, and had an entree to the Emperor's Court in St. Petersburg. For the Russian-American Fur Company, De Rezanov wanted a royal charter such as the British had given the East India Company. He negotiated first with Catherine the Great, who soon thereafter died, then with the new ruler, Emperor Paul. Along with his charter, he became the imperial spokesman.

V. J. Boucher, writing in *Alaska Sportsman* magazine 30 years ago, describes what happened:

*To secure the regulating authority he could get no other way, Count Rezanov sought an imperial charter for the new company. In 1799 it was granted. A few years later Count Rezanov appeared at the seal islands. He knew beforehand that the vast flood of seal (and otter) skins, once an open sesame to the teas and silks of China, had dwindled to a trickle, despite the fact that less than twenty years had elapsed since the discovery of the Pribilof Islands.*

*The Count took a long and thoughtful look at the frazzled fraction which remained of the "mighty chorus" that, not so long before, had "dwarfed the breakers' song," and he issued three orders. No killing of seals for five years. No removal of seal skins from the islands for five years. Remove half the transplanted Aleut crewmen entirely from the islands.*

*The third order was prompted by the fact that, throughout the Russian tenure of the Pribilofs, the sealing personnel subsisted almost entirely on seal meat.*

*The sea otter fishery was continued with Rezanov's approval, but method was substituted for the previous madness. All the sea otter coast from Prince William Sound to the tip of the Aleutians was divided into hunting districts and thereafter hunted on what might be called a two-three system. Each district was hunted hard for two years, then rested for three years.*

Toward the end of his reign, Gov. Baranov saw competition for the fur business increase steadily from the south. The Boston sea captains, the Yankee fur traders and others were taking hold all along the Pacific coast of North America. Baranov tried to cling to the sea otter profit by means of arrangements with American traders and hunters. He sent the magnificent Aleut hunters to work for the Americans and established a working base in California called Fort Rus, now known as Fort Ross. The hunters expertly plied their trade, even entering Spanish-controlled territory such as San Francisco Bay, where sea otters flourished in great numbers. In the nearly 30 years of operations in California, those hunting the sea otter for the Russians are believed to have taken about 50,000 of them, an amount estimated at a third of the entire sea otter population along the Spanish Pacific coast at that time.

The "Lord of Alaska" died in 1819, and after him the company managers were Russian navy officers whose main interests were exploration and navigation. Baranov's successors had nothing of the original magic, nor, tragically, had they brought with them Count De Rezanov's wisdom. When

profit turned to loss, Russia decided to get rid of the outpost. Great Britain was first approached; they declined. The United States was approached: Secretary of State William Seward expressed interest.

The hunting didn't end until Spanish California became Mexican. Mexican hunting regulations of the most protective kind were instituted and Capt. John Sutter bought the now-useless Fort Ross in 1841. Of course, the "protective" steps taken by the Mexicans didn't stop the slaughter; they merely specified who should carry it out.

The Russian presence had not gone from Fort Ross without a whimper. Although Spain claimed the Pacific coast as far north as Alaska, the government's physical capability ended at San Francisco, where there was a presidio (fort) and mission. Fort Ross was the Russian center for sea otter hunting; for sealing, they took up camp on the Farallon Islands. When they tried to hunt in territory where the Spaniards could detect them, they were treated harshly. They continued to hunt successfully the fur seals on the Farallon Islands off the California coast near San Francisco because these were outposts where the Spaniards did not go. Adele Ogden records that

*the Russians did not give up their Farallon outpost until years of wholesale killing exterminated the seal. Whereas the number taken in 1825 was 1,050, only fifty-four were received from the Farallones in 1833.*

*In contrast to sealing on island outposts, Russian otter hunting along the Spanish coast was not easy to continue on an independent basis. After 1813, the "Ilmen" came to Fort Ross with supplies and fifty Aleuts under (Vasilii Petrovich) Tarakanov. A hunting trip to the north was unsuccessful because of hostile natives. The vessel then sailed down the coast. For two days the Aleuts hunted around the Farallon Islands. Then the captain ordered them to slip into the (San Francisco) bay at night. Tarakanov tells what happened.*

*"The Aleuts did so and hunted all day, killing about 100 sea otters, but when we went to the beach on the south side to camp for the night we found soldiers stationed at all the springs who would not allow any one to take any water. At this the Aleuts became frightened and started back toward the ship which had remained outside. It was dark and some wind was blowing and two bidarkas (Aleut canoes) were capsized and the men, being tired with their day's work, could not save themselves."*

*The Aleuts who were capsized must have been seized by the Spaniards. In July, 1814, Kuskov (Russian governor) was petitioning Governor José Arguello for Kodiaks held at the presidio and explained that "They have done no wrong but were only compelled to save themselves from the surf in the bay at the port of San Francisco where they were captured."*

*The day of reckoning was coming. Some Russian sailors, eleven Alueuts and Tarakanov were ordered to get fresh meat. Seeing some cattle grazing in the hills near San Pedro (near Los Angeles), the men landed, but almost immediately they were surrounded by Spanish soldiers on horseback. The frightened sailors pushed off without waiting for Tarakanov or the Aleuts, who were tied together with ropes and taken on a two days' march to Santa Barbara. There they were destined to work for two years and more before being released.*

New orders then came from Madrid that trading with foreigners was to be limited to agricultural and manufactured products, "thus implying," the Ogden account tells us, "that the chief concern of Spanish authorities was to keep the marine wealth of the coast from the hands of the northerners."

When California became Mexican in 1821, the Russians immediately hoped to improve their hunting privileges. The new Mexican government realized that, at first, they could not maintain efficient patrols and halt poaching, so they allowed hunting by contract, extracting a profitable share. But by 1830 the Mexican policy had firmed up to the point that the Russians and Aleuts could hunt only as employees of the Mexicans, for it was now Mexican policy to nationalize all commerce.

*A white-faced sea otter uses kelp as ballast while he takes a look around.*

*Time to wake up from the afternoon nap.* ▶

*In the quiet waters of Monterey Harbor, no kelp sea belt is necessary for a floating nap.*

*Fort Ross, on the coast of Northern California, has been restored to look as it appeared when it was the base for Russian sea otter hunting. (California Department of Parks & Recreation.)*

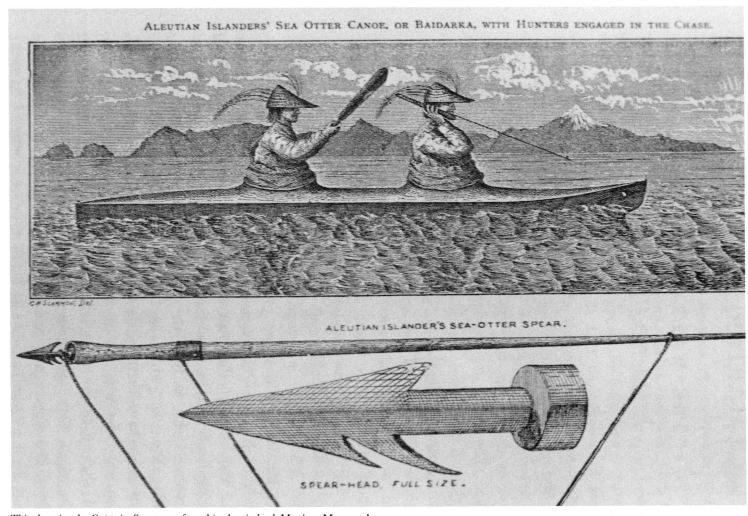

ALEUTIAN ISLANDERS' SEA OTTER CANOE, OR BAIDARKA, WITH HUNTERS ENGAGED IN THE CHASE.

ALEUTIAN ISLANDER'S SEA-OTTER SPEAR.

SPEAR-HEAD. FULL SIZE.

*This drawing by Captain Scammon from his classic book* Marine Mammals,
*shows the Aleuts hunting sea otters in their unique* baidarka, *with a close-up of
an otter-hunting spearhead. (Dover Publications).*

*A kelp bed off Monterey provides an ideal place for a nap between meals.*

*With his head poking out of the water, this sea otter has a quizzical look.*

# Counting Noses

The importance of the sea otter in the opening of the West—by enriching the merchants in Boston as well as the crowned heads in St. Petersburg and Madrid—cannot be underestimated. As California researcher Adele Ogden puts it, "The commercial opening of the Pacific Ocean was begun because of man's desire for the fur of an animal."

Because of the sea otter, the Manila galleons sailed with furs alongside cargoes of sandalwood from the Sandwich Islands. (Another abundant resource, the sandalwood tree used to cover the hills of Hawaii's Big Island. King Kamehameha allowed the harvest to continue to the point where there is now no such tree standing today. Only a sign indicates where they once flourished.) One Jose Fernandez is quoted as recording that along the shore of the harbor from San Francisco to the estuary of Santa Clara, "the ground appeared covered with black sheets due to the great quantity of otter which were there." None has been sighted there in this century.

Grinnell, a former University of California zoologist, quotes a reliable source who estimates that during the peak years of California sea otter hunting—between 1786 and 1868—more than 200,000 were killed. The hunting range extended from San Francisco Bay and the Farallon Islands south to Cedros Island off Baja California.

"The kill in San Francisco Bay alone was supposed to have reached as high as 700 to 800 a week," Grinnell recorded. "Within five years the Russians had taken 50,000, and at least 5,000 each year were taken thereafter until 1831."

In the early 1800s, various ships gathered fairly large cargoes of sea otter pelts off California for the Boston markets. One ship, the *O'Cain*, had 1,800 pelts from its 1803 voyage, and in the season of 1806–07, harvested a total of 4,819. In 1831 a hunting party at Santa Rosa Island took 75 sea otters "in a few weeks."

The sea otter is a fast learner. Californians and the Yankees, like the members of Bering's crew, learned that the sea otter quickly found out that these upright, strange-smelling creatures meant trouble. Russians armed with firearms had little better luck. The natives of the far north, however, knew how to hunt the sea otter and everything else in their world. They became masters of the aquatic hunt which few other people, including the Indian native to California, could match. The Aleuts referred to the sea otter as "our brother" because they both had mastered survival in the Arctic regions, but that did not prevent them from committing fratricide.

These natives of the north included Oonangans, who lived on the westernmost part of the Aleutian chain, and the Koniags, who lived in the Kodiak area. The Russians lumped them all together as Aleuts. In the eastern parts lived Tlingits and Haidas, known collectively as the Kolosh. The Russians were able to dominate and enslave the Aleuts, but the Kolosh shot back.

Because the Russians failed as sea-otter hunters, they pressed the Aleuts into service. In the early days the *promyschleniki* appreciated the talents of these native people and laid aside their own hunting equipment. They forced the Aleut hunters to work for them; they did this by taking women and children prisoner and forcing the men to hunt. If a hunter made a poor showing, he was tortured or, occasionally, shot. In an issue of *Earthlines/Tidelines*, the Alaska Geographic Society stated that "within 50 years after the first Russians came, the Aleutian chain was like a trail of blood. About 150,000 sea otters had been killed ... Except for few scattered groups in out-of-the-way places, the sea otters disappeared. And the Aleut population—by the Russians' own count—had tragically and unbelievably fallen through massacre and disease from an estimated 20,000 people to less than 2,000."

Capt. Scammon's book provides the best eyewitness descriptions of sea-otter hunting:

*About the sea-board of Upper and Lower California, Cedros, San Geronimo, Guadalupe, San Nicolas, and San Miguel Islands, have been regarded as choice places to pursue them; and farther northward, off Cape Blanco, on the Oregon coast, and Point Grenville and Gray's Harbor, along the coast of Washington Territory. At the present day, considerable numbers are taken by whites and Indians about those northern grounds. Thence, to the northward and westward, come a broken coast and groups of islands, where the animals were, in times past, hunted by the employees of the Hudson's Bay Company and Russian-American Company, and where they are still pursued by the natives inhabiting those rock-bound shores. These interesting mammals are gregarious, and are frequently seen in bands numbering from fifty up to hundreds.*

The Captain describes how the Aleuts, who were essentially Russian serfs at this period, carried out the hunt:

*The Aleutians, dressed in their water-proof garments, made from the intestines of seals, wedge themselves into their* baidarkas

*(which are constructed with a light, wooden frame, and covered with walrus or seal skin), and, donning their hunting caps, plunge through the surf that dashes high along the crags, and, with almost instinctive skill, reach the less turbulent ground-swell that heaves in every direction. These aquatic men are so closely confined by the narrow build of their boats, and keeping motion with them, too, that their appearance suggests the idea that some undescribed marine monster had just emerged from the depths below. Once clear of the rocks, however, the hunters watch diligently for the Otters. The first man that gets near one darts his spear, then throws up his paddle by way of signal; all the other boats forming a circle around him, at some distance. The wounded animal dives deeply, but soon returns to the surface, near some one of the* baidarkas *forming the circle. Again the hunter that is near enough hurls his spear and elevates his paddle, and again the ring is formed as before. In this way the chase is continued until the capture is made. As soon as the animal is brought on shore, the two oldest hunters examine it, and the one whose spear is found nearest the head is entitled to the prize.*

Capt. Scammon comments on the results of uncontrolled hunting off the lower Pacific coast and in the Aleutians:

*The number of Sea Otter skins taken annually is not definitely known, but from the most authentic information we can obtain, the aggregate for the past three years has been five thousand, one thousand of which came from the Kurile Islands; and, valuing each skin at fifty dollars, amounts to the sum of two hundred and fifty thousand dollars.*

*Whether these very valuable fur animals have decreased in*

*numbers within the past few years, is questionable. The hunting of them on the coast of the California is no longer profitable for more than two or three hunters, and we believe of late some seasons have passed without any one legitimately engaging in the enterprise; notwithstanding, off Point Grenville, which is an old hunting-ground, sixty Otters were taken by only three hunters in the summer of 1868 — a great annual increase over many past years. It is said the Russian-American Company restricted the number taken by the Aleutian Islanders, from whom the chief supply was obtained, in order to perpetuate the stock. Furthermore, may it not be that these sagacious animals have fled from those places on the coasts of Californias where they were so constantly pursued, to some more isolated haunt, and now remain unmolested?*

Capt. Scammon was apparently remembering his discovery of the gray whales' "hiding places" in the lagoons of Baja California. As we know, the southern sea otters did have a hiding place of sorts, but not enough of them remained to allow reproduction to continue at the rate it did in the north. That small band of holdouts discovered in 1938 off Big Sur, where the steep cliffs provided a natural barrier between sea otter and man, was the sole surviving raft of any consequence. It is interesting to note that the Captain knew of Count De Rezanov's "crop rotation" plan and that he credits it in part with the survival of the northern sea otter. Throughout his writings, very slight twinges of conscience and admiration for the capabilities — if not the intelligence! — of the animals he himself pursued keep popping up.

Adele Ogden describes how the hunt was carried out off the two Californias. "Hunting methods of the American

gunman differed from the mass methods used by the Aleut with his spear," she wrote. "Although some shooting was done from the land, most hunting was pursued at sea by small groups of from three to five men."

She notes that these groups usually brought along Hawaiians to paddle the canoes and then to dive in and retrieve the sea otter. The *kanakas*, as these hunters were called, were highly regarded for their aquatic prowess but, she says, "gradually California Indians were employed more frequently, and, according to Nidever, in paddling 'they soon superseded the Kanakas.'"

About the actual hunt she writes:

*When putting out to sea, the gunman took his position at the prow of the boat. Near at hand were two or three favorite rifles, with perhaps a musket or two, and a plentiful supply of ammunition.*

*The common way to hunt was in groups of three canoes, in each of which were three men, a gunman and two rowers. At sea a triangular formation was kept. One canoe pulled in advance with the others following in place on each quarter stern. As soon as an otter was seen within rifle shot — which, according to Phelps, was from seventy-five to one hundred yards — the hunter immediately fired. The nearest boat followed the wake of the fleeing animal, the others falling into proper position with the object of keeping the animal inside the triangle. Standing in the bow of his boat, with his rifle to his shoulder, the hunter fired every time the otter rose to the surface or breached. It was not work for the novice.*

Writing in 1940, she observes:

*An environment of cracking gun reports and showers of musket balls is not conducive to the preservation of the sea otter species and accounted for this rapid decrease in California after the 1830's. The extinction of the species along the California coast was considered inevitable until a short time ago. In the 1890's and early in the twentieth century until 1917, occasional otters were seen and shot between San Luis Obispo and Monterey and around the islands opposite Upper and Lower California. Fortunately, some of the long, lonely stretches of the California coast have served as quiet havens where a few of these rare species have been able to live their natural life, undisturbed by man.*

It may seem that the Russians have been made the villains in the near-extinction of the sea otter, but this has not been my purpose. The Russians were merely the first, and in some ways the most exotic, of the hunters. If they had not already made the richness of the sea otter pelt known in both China and St. Petersburg, then someone else—such as Great Britain's Capt. James Cook—would have. In fact, Cook alerted the Boston sea captains and merchants to the value of the pelts. Because of them, others, including the French, entered the picture.

Hunting methods have become more humane over the years, but these methods are just as deadly. Bering's men clubbed the otters to death in much the same manner as the Canadian and Norwegian hunters, for instance, go after the seals in eastern Canada today. The Aleuts started off by clubbing otters while they were asleep on the rocky shores of Alaska.

Adele Ogden writes:

*In California and in certain places in the North Pacific, nets spread out on the kelp beds, snares, and clubs were used. On the Northwest Coast during bad weather, when the animals sought shelter in large numbers along the rocks, natives would sometimes under cover of a howling gale dispatch them with heavy wood clubs. Padre Luís Sales described an interesting method—which may have been used only by California Indians since no known voyager to the Northwest has mentioned it. When the parent otter left its young on the surface of the water, which it did only when it dived for food, the Indian hunter would slip up and tie a cord to the foot of the baby. Fastened to the cord, close to the body of the animal, would be placed a couple of fishhooks. Retiring in his canoe to a short distance, the Indian would pull his cord and thus hurt the small otter so that he would cry. The mother would rush to the rescue and be easily approached, either because she was occupied in freeing her offspring or because she herself would become caught in the line and hooks.*

Just as we have the Russian Count De Rezanov to thank for bringing a certain amount of sense to the ceaseless slaughter of the sea otter in the north, two Mexican officials should be noted for their efforts as well. When the West Coast was under Spanish rule, outsiders were not permitted to hunt the otters. Baranov's men were successful working out of Fort Ross only because there was no effective Spanish military presence north of San Francisco. Two years after Spanish America became Mexican, a licensing system was introduced. To a certain extent, both the Spanish ban and the Mexican licensing produced much the same results as the American Prohibition on alcohol did: bootleggers. The first governor, José Maria Echeandía, and later his successor, Manuel Victoria, decreed that baby otters could not be killed, although hunting by license was allowed. A number of abuses in the licensing system eventually resulted in the decree that only citizens of Mexico—including California—could hunt.

Kenyon believes that in its northern range the sea otter population in 1740 was "probably between 100,000 and 150,000 animals... The number of sea otters taken during 170 years of unregulated exploitation is not recorded but probably did not much exceed one-half million animals... The total world population in 1911, when exploitation of the sea otter was halted, probably numbered between 1,000 and 2,000 animals." In 1965 Kenyon said that the world population was then estimated to be between 32,000 and 35,000. Ten years later Kenyon stated that the Alaskan population was well over 100,000 and he quoted a figure for the southern sea otter between 1,357 and 1,537.

In *Earthlines/Tidelines*, the Alaska Geographic Society records that

*by 1867, when the United States bought Alaska from Russia, the [northern] sea otters had built back to around 100,000—maybe more.*

*The U.S. also tried to limit the hunt to the Native people. But it was a hopeless task. With sea otter pelts bringing as much as $1,000 apiece on London markets, everybody got in the act. French, British, Canadian and American fur hunters swarmed into the area, bringing out 5,000 sea otters or more each year. Steadily the numbers dropped.*

*Finally in 1910, when only 24 pelts were taken, so few sea otters were left they were hardly worth hunting.*

*The following year all high seas hunting of sea otters was banned by international agreement. In 1913 the Territory of Alaska passed a law protecting them inside the three-mile limit, and the Aleutian Island National Refuge was established to save the few scattered survivors that were left.*

In 1913 California passed a law making it illegal "to take or possess" a sea otter without a special permit.

As *Earthlines/Tidelines* recorded, the result was that "given peace and lack of human predators, the tough little sea otter proved it could ride out the tide of human destruction as well as the crashing waves in which it plays. Servicemen stationed in the lonely Aleutians during World War II spotted sleek heads bobbing in the surf. Excited biologists picked up their surveys again and were delighted to find that the sea otters were increasing at the rate of about five percent a year."

For a variety of reasons, ranging from food availability to the human factor, the sea otter has fared much better in its northern habitat than it has in its southern range. Sea otters seem to thrive in splendid isolation!

*This otter displays her flipper hind feet, used to control swimming, contrasting strongly with the handlike forepaws.*

*These white-faced sea otters rest at identical angles.*

*A group of otters frolic in the surf.*

*After a nap, this sea otter seems to grin with satisfaction.*

*Perils North and South*

Sea otters are at risk today throughout sea otter country, from north to south, from Alaska and the Kuriles to California. The existence of the sea otter and other marine mammals bearing coveted fur coats has been threatened through history. The hunt for the fur alone nearly wiped out otters and fur seals. The search for oil decimated both elephant seals and a variety of whales. (Even though the search for oil has moved to the ocean bottom, marine mammals are still imperiled because of it.) "Incidental deaths," caused when marine mammals and sea birds get caught in nets and drown, create new hazards for marine life. Legal protection has been imposed in many instances, but the outlaw, the poacher and the warped mind still pose a threat.

The fur industry 's exploitation of marine mammals caused governments to take steps to halt the extinction of several species. Although the motivation behind these new laws was somewhat cynical and was intended to preserve a "harvestable" population, the end result has been the preservation of what would otherwise be a doomed species.

The Alaska Geographic Society publishes a handsome quarterly called *Alaska Geographic*. The publication is beautifully illustrated, carefully researched and precisely written. The third volume for the year 1982 was devoted to the famous fur seal islands, the Pribilofs. The international treaty of 1911, which halted the extinction of the sea otter and the fur seals, is recorded in it:

"Commercial exploitation of the northern fur seal began with the discovery of their breeding grounds. With the major fur source, sea otters, fast becoming scarce, Russian fur traders immediately turned their pursuits to the fur seal. In the early years of Russian control, fur seals were killed indiscriminately, with no regard for sex, age, or number taken. In the first year, 1786–87, more than 40,000 fur seal pelts were obtained, while the take of sea otter pelts was only 2,000."

In later years the steps taken to maintain a breeding stock of sea otters were applied to fur seals. When the United States annexed Alaska in 1867, further attempts were made to preserve the species, but for many years the attempts were unsuccessful. When sealing expanded to include the sea as well, a new threat was added. *Alaska Geographic* continues:

*As a commercial enterprise, pelagic sealing began in the late 1860s. Prior to this time, pelagic sealing was limited to Northwest Coast Indians using canoes and spears and, in some cases, gill nets. But this primitive subsistence activity soon turned into a business because of two innovations: the use of mother ships capable of transporting canoes and hunters many miles offshore, and the use of firearms. In the pelagic sealing heyday (1889–1909), more than 600,000 seals were killed, exceeding or nearly exceeding the number harvested on land every year. This depredation was disastrous to the Pribilof herd for three reasons: many seals were lost due to sinking or wounding, most seals taken were breeding and pregnant females feeding at sea, and loss of a female subsequently meant the death of her pup from starvation on the rookery.*

Eventually the U.S. Government took over all sealing rights, which caused some problems with Great Britain because of Canadian sealers. Finally, "in 1911, representatives from the United States, Great Britain (for Canada),

Russia, and Japan met to form a treaty which resulted in the North Pacific Seal Convention. Under the terms of the convention, pelagic sealing was prohibited by nationals of the four governments, except for aboriginals using primitive methods. In addition, the convention provided for sharing of fur seal pelts between participating members."

*Alaska Geographic,* in the second volume for 1981, carries this account:

*By the 1900s, because of unlimited hunting allowed by the United States, sea otters were nearly gone: estimates today are that perhaps 2,000 were left. In 1911 sea otters were given complete protection.*

*Today sea otters, still under complete protection, have recovered to nearly their original numbers. Biologists believe that there are overpopulations of the animals in some areas where mortality is high from malnutrition and disease.*

*In 1968 John Vania, a wind-bronzed marine mammal biologist for the Alaska Department of Fish and Game, strolled down an aisle at the Seattle Fur Exchange with a 7-foot-long rich dark fur draped over his shoulder. The 50 or 60 buyers there converged on the fur, but none could identify it.*

*They were experts, and from all around the world. They carefully examined the soft, rich pelt. It was like the finest velvet with a one-inch pile. They shook the pelt; it shimmered like fire. They blew into the lustrous depths to separate the fibers to see the skin, but the fur was too dense: they could see no skin. Fine, silvered guard hairs, scarcely longer than the fur fibers, sprinkled the rich, brown fur, counterpointing the luxurious darkness. They brushed its softness against their cheeks. The fur was clearly of the finest quality and of great value.*

*The pelt was, of course, a sea otter fur, and Vania was representing the state of Alaska in trying to determine if there was still a market for sea otter fur. He quickly learned that buyers were eager for the return of the sea otter furs to the market.*

*In 1967 Alaska announced it would market 1,000 sea otter furs in 1968 — animals that were biologically surplus in areas of sea otter overpopulation.*

*Alaska did market a total of about 2,500 sea otter furs over a period of several years. The fur industry showed much interest and paid well for them. Alaska biologists intended to harvest only the surplus animals, to thin the main herds for their own health. A long-term, scientifically managed program was planned on that basis.*

*But in 1972 the federal government was given responsibility for management of all marine mammals in the U.S., and since that time, less work has been done with Alaska's sea otters. In 1973, the last year the state of Alaska counted sea otters, their population was calculated to be between 100,000 and 125,000.*

A lack of state funds slowed down the Alaska harvest plan in 1970, but the passage of the Marine Mammal Protection Act of 1972 ended any possibility of immediately reviving the harvesting. There are provisions allowing individual states to assume management of species protected by the Act, but this takes time. James H. Hogue, special agent-in-charge, Division of Law Enforcement of the United States Fish and Wildlife Service in Alaska, has predicted the return of the harvesting of sea otters in Alaska "under very controlled conditions."

I asked Hogue what perils the sea otter now faces in Alaska and he rewarded me with this comprehensive account:

*For several years after the passage of the Marine Mammal Protection Act (MMPA) there were conflicting opinions as to whether Alaska Natives could legally take sea otters for subsistence purposes. A recent opinion rendered by the Department of Interior's Regional Solicitor, Anchorage, Alaska, states that Alaska Natives can take and utilize sea otters for subsistence purposes. A limited number of sea otters are now being harvested by Alaska Natives in Alaskan waters. As with other marine mammals, the hides must first be made into authentic Native articles or handicraft or clothing before they can be sold or transferred to a non-Native.*

*In recent years there has been a very limited illegal harvest of sea otters for sale on the black market with prices ranging up to $2,000 per pelt. This illegal activity has been held to a minimum by the use of undercover agents and informants and with the excellent cooperation of the U.S. Attorney's office and the Federal Courts in Alaska. All subjects apprehended for taking or dealing illegally in sea otters have been convicted. Penalties have ranged up to $10,000 fines and six months imprisonment. Individuals involved range from the "old-time trapper" to those just trying to make a fast buck and include Alaska Natives and foreign nationals.*

*In many areas of Alaska where sea otter populations have reached all-time highs, many people believe sea otters are decimating crab, clam and bottomfish populations. As a result, commercial fishermen and others are killing sea otters and not harvesting the pelts. This type of illegal take is extremely difficult to control.*

The sea otters face perils along the coast of California, too, although the population has not returned to anywhere near the point it enjoyed before the hunters arrived. For a variety of reasons, it is doubtful that it ever could, even with government help. In Alaska there are natural barriers to attack by man, including areas of relative isolation where the sea otters can grow unmolested by humans. The sea otter has not reestablished itself in California as happily as in Alaska because there are few such isolated sites. The original one at Big Sur is one of them.

California is also much more a melting pot of races, cultures and attitudes; this sort of freedom for humans has resulted in problems for nature. The basic problem is a difference in culture. In some parts of the world, conservation practices are unknown. Wild animals are thought to have been created by the gods to provide for man. Age and gender of an animal make no more difference to a hungry hunter than they did to the early fur trappers.

Six Laotian refugees taking up residence in Fresno were fined a total of $5,720 in 1983 for illegally hunting does and fawns. An uproar had also begun because other immigrants were fishing California's bays with gill nets, resulting in the "incidental catch" of sea otters, aquatic birds, sea lions, seals and dolphins.

In California, the gill net probably produced more fireworks than anything else. Fishermen refer to it as a "curtain" because it is placed between the ocean bottom and the surface and can trap anything that comes along. Some nets extend as much as a mile and a half. They are used to catch certain types of fish that attempt to swim through the nets and get caught by their gills in them. Unfortunately, birds diving for fish also get caught in them, as do marine mammals.

In 1982 the governor of California signed a bill limiting the use of gill nets close to shore in the Monterey Bay area; the law was applied temporarily elsewhere, notably off the

San Francisco area. The law was strengthened in 1984. In both instances, lawmakers took action after outcries of rage erupted from a variety of conservation groups ranging from the Audubon Society to the Friends of the Sea Otter. Under this law arrests have been made and fines imposed.

Some fishermen consider the sea lions a threat to their livelihood and shoot them; one Monterey Bay individual was found guilty of shooting *at* a sea lion, not necessarily killing it. Under the terms of the Marine Mammal Protection Act he was fined $15,000 after appealing a lower fine. Sea otters are considered enemies of shellfishery interests, but I know of only one conviction for shooting a sea otter in the last quarter century. Sea otter bodies with bullets in them have, however, been found washed up on California's shores, for the most part in the otters' southern range.

The sea otter faces even more insidious threats from far more powerful interests. Fish and Wildlife biologist Glenn VanBlaricom wrote an important paper in 1982 entitled, "Relationships of Sea Otters to Living Marine Resources in California: A New Perspective." Consider this statement by VanBlaricom:

"The sea otter population in California presently numbers less than 2,000 animals and occupies a small portion of its original range. The population has not grown in recent years. . . . In spite of their tenuous status, however, sea otters are at the center of ongoing disputes involving impacts on shellfisheries and offshore petroleum development. As a result, regulatory agencies have found it difficult to develop a management scheme for sea otters that is consistent with scientific data and also satisfies the full range of public concern."

The key phrase, "satisfies the full range of public concern," includes those who wish to allow the sea otter to survive, those who would rather harvest shellfish, and those who would take a chance with the otters' survival for the sake of petrodollars.

From a discussion of the shellfishery, VanBlaricom moves to

*the threat of increased offshore oil development and transport to the sea otter population in California. Contamination of the pelage by oil disrupts the thermoregulatory system of the sea otter and can produce fatal hypothermia . . . Over 100 sea otters died as a result of spillage of gasoline and diesel fuel in the Kurile Islands of the Soviet Union in 1964 . . . Development of offshore petroleum resources in California is now expanding rapidly. Three active oil tanker terminals presently exist within the current range of the sea otter in California, and proposed and existing federal and state sales of offshore oil leases may soon create overlaps between offshore drilling sites and sea otter range . . . Available data suggests that wind and current patterns along the shore of central California could cause a large oil slick to spread rapidly through the sea otter range . . .*

*In response to the threat of oil spills, the U.S. Fish and Wildlife Service designated the California sea otter population as "threatened" in 1977, pursuant to the Endangered Species Act of 1973 as amended . . . Thus, the California sea otter population is the focus of dispute between conservationists who favor increased protection, and energy interests who see development of California's offshore petroleum resources as an important step toward reduced dependence on foreign imports.*

It is important to note that, as VanBlaricom states, the California sea otter population is the one placed under the protection of the Endangered Species Act. (The only problem with the Endangered Species Act is that it requires reexamination of a designation every five years, which can create political maneuvering and mischief.)

VanBlaricom and fellow Fish and Wildlife Service biologist Ronald J. Jameson wrote further on the subject of oil spill threats in the March 19, 1982, issue of *Science,* a publication of the American Association for the Advancement of Science. The article, "Lumber Spill in Central California Waters: Implications for Oil Spills and Sea Otters," used an offshore lumber spill to observe the drift and distance of an oil spill as it might affect the sea otters' habitat:

"A large quantity of lumber was spilled in the ocean off central California during the winter of 1978, and it spread through most of the range of the threatened California sea otter population within four weeks. The movement rates of lumber were similar to those of oil slicks observed elsewhere. These observations indicate that a major oil spill could expose significant numbers of California sea otters to oil contamination."

Their study notes that while the sea otters tend to remain within one kilometer of the shoreline, "data from drift card and bottle studies indicate . . . within 75 kilometers of shore, onshore movements of floating materials during winter is aided by strong southerly or southwesterly winds often associated with Pacific frontal systems and by milder southwesterly winds that frequently prevail for one or two days after the passage of fronts. Propagation of meanders and eddies from the shoreward edge of the Cali-

fornia Current may promote the onshore transport of floating materials during any season."

They concluded that "two to three major oil spills are expected to result from oil production on the outer continental shelf."

Oil spills *do* take place despite precautions to prevent them. Ships plying the coastal sea lanes have been known to pump their bilges despite laws to the contrary, and from these, contamination can also result. On January 28, 1969, a well off Santa Barbara blew out, fouling the beaches in one of America's most beautiful places. During the 10 days before the well was capped, thousands of barrels of oil flowed unchecked into the sea and killed an uncounted number of birds and marine mammals. While drilling techniques have improved since then, the spectre of mechanical and human error remains.

Other petroleum catastrophes in recent years are reminders of what can happen. *Ixtoc I* blew in the Gulf of Mexico on June 3, 1979, and in 295 uncontrolled days it lost 140 million gallons of oil into the sea. March 16, 1978, the largest supertanker disaster to date occurred off Port Sall, France, when the *Amoco Cádiz* was grounded and lost 68 million gallons of oil; this spill soiled 200 miles of French coastline—a distance equivalent to the entire range of the California sea otter.

The April 1984 near-grounding of the tanker *Sealift Pacific,* which, laden with more than 6 million gallons of diesel fuel, drifted helplessly to within a mile and a half of the shore in the heart of the sea otter range off Big Sur, brought another chilling reminder of the daily threat of a tanker spill.

International efforts attempted to halt war-related oil leaks in the Persian Gulf in 1983, but nothing could be done before hundreds of dolphins died.

The likelihood of a similar disaster within the range of the California sea otter is the reason for the urgency in getting a segment of this sea otter population translocated outside the parts of California waters where an oil spill could wipe them out. Their miraculous escape from extinction still hangs in delicate balance.

*Sea otters spend most of their lives floating on their backs — not always their own!*

*To achieve perfect comfort, this sea otter keeps one half of himself out of the water and one half in.*

*This cautious sea otter hangs onto his rock with one paw while he checks out the surrounding waters.*

*Following page: A yawn doesn't necessarily indicate boredom in the otter world.* ▶

*Page 54: A white face does not mean the otter is a senior citizen; white facial fur can come within a year or two.*

*Mother sea otter seems to have a white mustache, but her baby couldn't care less.*

# *Behind the Controversy*

U nless some remedial actions are taken, competition between otters and humans will intensify. This in turn will heighten animosity toward sea otters and lead to increased illegal killing."

This chilling sentence comes from the Department of the Interior's 1983 annual review of the status of various marine mammals coming under the protection of the Marine Mammal Protection Act of 1972. This quotation refers to certain parts of Alaska, where the sea otter has gained dramatically in its brush with extinction. The sea otter in its southern (California) range has not been so fortunate.

There seems to be no way to tell a man whose family has fished a certain ground for a number of generations that he has to share those fishing grounds with the mammals that share the sea with the fish. He can react rather drastically and outside the law if he feels his own rights are under fire.

Among those with whom I discussed the sea otter while writing this book was Earl E. Ebert, the senior marine biologist at the California Department of Fish & Game's Marine Culture Laboratory, located roughly halfway between Monterey and Big Sur on a narrow shelf of land west of the Coastal Highway.

He stated the various points of view concerning both otters and shellfisheries:

"From data and observations made over a 30-year period, it is obvious that shellfisheries such as those for abalone, clams and sea urchins cannot co-exist with the sea otter. Yet this issue continues to be debated today.

"Unquestionably, the sea otter is a valuable member of our offshore community, esthetically, perhaps, without peer.

However, shellfisheries also warrant consideration in the planning and management of our nearshore living resources. All too often, environmentalists adopt what I refer to as an aboriginal point of view in seeking a return to what existed historically, rather than examining, or considering, the ecology of mankind in our contemporary world, which I believe is more realistic."

"A compromise is in order," Ebert declared as the interview went on. That compromise is to maintain "a viable sea otter population along the central California coast, but to permit the continuance of shellfisheries beyond this region via zonal management."

In a letter written September 14, 1983 and submitted to the Department of the Interior's Director of the Fish and Wildlife Service, a letter that expresses the extent of its findings and recommendations in the mid-1980s, the Marine Mammal Commission states: "The southern sea otter population, which had been increasing at about 5 percent per year throughout the 1960s, apparently has not grown and may have declined in the last several years."

That letter, a report of findings by the Marine Mammal Commission's Committee of Scientific Advisors' Sea Otter Working Group, also claims that "establishing one or more sea otter colonies outside the present California sea otter range could adversely affect certain commercial and recreational shellfish fisheries, and it is generally recognized that some type of zonal management ultimately will be required to effectively protect both sea otters and valuable shellfish resources."

On the surface it may appear that this statement contradicts previous stands to establish a safe refuge for the

California sea otter population. The "adverse effect" on certain fisheries refers to one private mariculture enterprise already established at San Nicolas Island. The introduction of sea otters there would "adversely affect" this undertaking, unless the shellfish are protected by wire enclosures, as is done elsewhere. However, mariculture was introduced at San Nicolas under a Department of Fish & Game permit *after* the department warned the entrepreneurs that the Island was actively being considered as a site for sea otter translocation, and that the fact that a shellfishery was to be introduced would not influence the department's decision whether or not to relocate otters there.

In 1982 the Department of the Interior approved the Southern Sea Otter Recovery Plan. In 1984, they proceeded with action that makes San Nicolas a likely site to receive sea otters. Even should both sides in the shellfishery–sea otter controversy reach agreement, it will take some time to implement the plan.

The Fish and Wildlife Service will have to carry out the plan, the basic goal of which is to establish a colony of sea otters where they do not currently exist. This would be done in the hope that a new breeding colony would allow the present population to increase.

Establishment of a new colony, according to Interior's report, "will reduce the possibility of decimation of the existing population from an oil spill."

This leads to the crux of the controversy. In the early stages of the recovery of the California sea otter population, just about everyone was happy. Then the sea otter, in part thanks to federal and state protection, started to enlarge its range.

The basis for much of the alarm is to be found in the marketplace. According to a California Department of Fish & Game report released in 1984, fishermen were paid $2.95 a pound for red abalone, $1.53 a pound for Dungeness crab and 32¢ a pound for whole sea urchins, with bonuses added depending on the roe content. The same report stated that fishermen receive $3.75 a pound for California spiny lobster, but only 60¢ a pound for octopus and 19¢ a pound for squid. Both urchin and fish roe are popular in Asian markets; in Japan herring roe brought $10 to $12 a pound. The Japanese also paid up to $30 a pound for urchin roe. By the time these fish reach the dinner table or are served at a restaurant, prices will reach whatever the market will bear.

In areas where clams provide the shellfisheries with a good income, the sea otter is considered the enemy. On the other hand, in areas such as the Monterey Peninsula, the sea otter is considered an important tourist attraction.

While the shellfishermen and mariculturists were not consoled by the report, Estes and VanBlaricom, in their study of shellfisheries quoted earlier, found that the Pismo clam can survive to a certain extent in the presence of otters. The problem is that the numbers are not commercially viable nor are the clams always of legal size. They describe the sea otters' long-range impact on the Pismo clam, which reaches sexual maturity and starts reproducing at a size smaller than a sea otter will eat: "For unknown reasons, sea otters are apparently unwilling or unable to eat clams smaller than about 6 or 7 centimeters in length. Thus, some reproductive clams survive in the presence of sea otters."

More recently, California Fish & Game's Jack Ames cautioned me: "We have to be careful about talking about elimination of a fishery. A *fishery* may be eliminated, but the *clam* is not eliminated. It's the new balance in the presence of sea otters but, some recruitment is going on all the time. Let's be careful not to imply that the species is in trouble. We must remember that these (clam) populations would never have been developed if the sea otter had not been (nearly) exterminated."

Mollusc populations, along with the numbers of a variety of species, have never been constant throughout history. Executive director of Friends of the Sea Otter, Carol Fulton, pointed out in the August/September 1979 issue of *CNR* (California Natural Resources), a publication of the California Wildlife Federation: "The otter has just reached Pismo, yet the number of clams has been declining since the turn of the century: from a bag limit of 200 clams in the early 1900s, the limit has been reduced to 10 by 1948, the same year the commercial clam fishery was prohibited due to lack of clams left to support it."

In that same article, statements offered in balance were made by California Fish & Game's Tim Farley. He was asked, "Do you believe the otter or man is primarily responsible for the decreasing numbers of shellfish along the California coast?" His answer in part was:

*Man has undoubtedly impacted California's shellfish resources. Exploitation of a virgin population normally results in a lower population level. This is partially compensated for by increased success of reproduction. Shellfish population levels are also influenced by environmental variables, and certain species seem to fluctuate cyclically.*

*Within the sea otters' range, however, there is little doubt that their presence controls populations upon which they feed. Urchins and abalones are limited to cryptic individuals out of reach of foraging otters, and Pismo clams are reduced to those below 2 inches in size. Fortunately, there are sufficient numbers that remain to reproduce themselves. Unfortunately, recreational or commercial use of these resources is precluded.*

To which Carol Fulton added:

*The decreasing size of the shellfish all along the California coast, and California's expanding human population, leave little doubt that increasing human pressures are primarily responsible for diminishing shellfish.*

*Sea otters eat shellfish, but will never wipe out a population . . . Certainly the depletion of shellfish in many areas outside the otter's range cannot be considered the responsibility of the California sea otter: South of the otters' range, both in Baja, Mexico, and around Santa Barbara, the commercial abalone fisheries declined 43 percent between 1968 and 1973–74 . . . We would like to see a natural balance restored between man, otter and shellfish, but with the tremendous human pressures on shellfish populations today, this may not be possible.*

Estes and VanBlaricom comment: "There are both commercial and recreational facilities for most species. In some cases, landings from the recreational fisheries are thought to equal or exceed commercial landings. Yet often, usually for simple practical reasons, recreational fisheries are unmonitored or effectively unregulated."

There is obviously a need to maintain both commercial and recreational fisheries, just as room must also be maintained for the sea otter. The take from recreational fishing finds its way to the table; it is not wasted, and the enjoyment of consumption is often enhanced by the fact that the consumer caught the fare himself.

Clams, abalone or lobster are not in the strictest sense necessary; neither are sea otters. It is a question of finding a place for all. Those who go to sea to net the fish we eat, those who brave the depths to bring up shellfish, those who face storms to set traps for lobsters and retrieve them, all earn whatever they are paid.

Nor should the sea otters be eradicated to make the oceans safe for abalone. There has always been room for both. Nature's course is a seesawing action in which one species may enjoy a high while another battles a low.

The sea otter serves man commercially and spiritually. Even if he didn't, he is part of nature's cycle; who says he has to serve man to justify his existence?

*Following page: This otter keeps his rock tool handy while munching on a scallop.* ►

*A favorite California lunch for an otter is squid.*

*In Monterey, the squid lunch is called calamari.*

*Eating squid can be as messy as eating spaghetti!*

*This otter bangs a clam against the rock on her tummy to crack it open.*

*Clams are a favorite otter snack.*

*How about clams on the half shell?*

*How do you eat a sea urchin? Very carefully!*

# Home on the Range

The California sea otter expanded its range fairly rapidly after the animals were "rediscovered" in 1938. From the late 1970s on, both expansion of range and population growth seemed to slow. A large group of males established its presence near Santa Cruz and has remained there since the late 1970s.

Morro Bay and Pismo Beach have had scientific attention turned to them in recent years because sea otters have been competing with human clam diggers. The sea otters appear to have won. Laurence Laurent, a Department of Fish & Game marine biologist quoted by San Luis Obispo *Telegram-Tribune* in 1984, says that "the otter is only returning to his old domain. If he hadn't been taken away 150 years ago, there wouldn't have been the clams we had during the first half of this century. The otter is re-establishing himself and we're suffering and seeing consequences of that."

Laurent noted that even when the waters are churned up by offshore storms, sea otters have no problem diving to the bottom, finding a clam and returning to the surface. He stated he had seen the same thing in 1976, when he observed some early tests at the Diablo Canyon Nuclear Power Plant site. The water was so stirred up by the tests that it could be compared with a cataract, but the sea otters had no problems finding food.

"Even though visibility was zero, they still managed to find food. The same thing is true in the surf. Otters can find clams easily and, unlike people, don't have to rely on low tide," the *Telegram-Tribune* quoted him.

Sea otters locate their food more by the sense of touch, using both paws and whiskers, than by sight or smell.

Kenyon writes:

*Many observations indicate that the sea otter uses its forepaws primarily to gather food and that the tactile sense is important in locating food organisms. A captive female with good eyesight was offered food in a bucket about half full of turbid water. In one instance the bucket contained 200 small crabs* (Pachygrapsus), *4 blue mussels* (Mytilus edulis), *and a number of pebbles of various sizes. The otter had eaten both organisms before but showed a preference for mussels. When the bucket was presented to her, she immediately reached to the bottom with both forepaws, her chin on the edge of the bucket, and within a few seconds retrieved the four mussels. She made no attempt to place her head in the bucket or to look into it. Thus, she demonstrated a high reliance on her tactile sense in selecting the mussels from among pebbles and crabs.*

Kenyon also states that otters in the wild usually forage for food only during daylight hours, but that mothers can and will go after food during the hours of darkness because of the added feeding responsibilities. They appear to enjoy the same rate of success hunting after dark as during daylight.

Sea otters apparently do not use their teeth to help in gathering food. Their teeth are designed for chewing, not grasping. Kenyon observed otters catching fish with their forepaws: once on the surface they put the fish head in their mouth to kill it by crushing it. He offers evidence that they use their ever-present rock as a tool below water to dislodge abalone rather than use their teeth. On the surface they will place the rock on their chest and bang a clam or a large crab claw against it to crack the shell.

Kenyon leads us to another important facet of the sea otters' lifestyle with this statement: "Observations indicate that the sea otter subsists only on benthic organisms. Wide, deep passes between islands, which prevent bottom feeding, appear to act as a barrier to the spread of sea otter populations."

Marine biologists believe that depth and expanses of vacant sandy areas act as natural barriers to the expansion of the sea otter's range. The deepest a sea otter will dive for food is about 20 fathoms—120 feet. They are obviously more comfortable in much shallower water. I have watched the resident sea otters in Monterey harbor dive repeatedly for crab and clams; inside the Marina the water is 10 to 12 feet at its deepest. The otters take 15 to 30 seconds to go to the bottom, where there appears to be an unending supply of Washington and gaper (also called horseneck) clams, and return to the surface.

Off Point Lobos the average depth is between 70 and 100 feet—until the Carmel Submarine Canyon which, like the nearby Monterey Canyon, goes down 10,000 feet. Similar conditions exist off the shores of Alaska.

Ames concurs that these natural barriers keep the southern sea otter population from expanding either north or south. South of Morro Bay, he says, there are expanses of sand that appear barren of the type of food the otters want. At the same time there are fish, and fishing activity discourages otters. At the northern end of the range, just beyond Santa Cruz, the otters not only have to run the gauntlet of gill nets but the white shark population picks up dramatically. Ames estimated that one in 10 known otter deaths has been the result of shark bite; otters' bodies have been recovered with teeth from a great white shark embedded in them.

Despite this there is no evidence that a white shark has ever actually consumed a sea otter. None has ever been found in the stomach of a shark dissected by scientists. (Much the same is true for humans. Ebert mentions a theory that sharks do not like human prey. Sharks tend to snap at whatever arouses their curiosity; swimmers, surfers and divers who have been bitten by sharks have not been consumed.)

"Ten years ago I would have expected them to push on north," Ames told me, "on to San Francisco. But sharks may be one of the reasons they don't get beyond Año Nuevo." He listed four limiting factors: the sandy expanse barrier, the gill nets, sharks and shootings (which tend to take place at the southern limit of the range where fishing activity is the heaviest).

California Fish & Game biologists aren't especially sympathetic to the enlargement of the sea otters' range because of the impact on shellfisheries. They feel there is room for both, but only provided the range of the sea otter is "managed," Ames told me:

"It is my view that if we are talking about getting them to a place where they can survive, their present range is adequate. There is no question that at one time they were in real bad trouble. People didn't know they existed."

The first attempt to create more habitats for sea otters was occasioned by the atomic bomb. The Atomic Energy Commission planned to set off a bomb in Alaska, Jameson explained to me, and "in mitigation of this the Alaska Department of Fish and Game worked out an agreement to translocate some sea otters . . . this was one of the earliest attempts and it was funded by the AEC."

Attempts at relocating sea otters, the main purpose of which "was to reestablish them in their historic range," Jameson told me, were not successful. Kenyon was among those who participated in these pioneering attempts. He said these early failures were "because of insufficient knowledge of the sea otters' needs in captivity." Thirty-five animals were captured at Amchitka in 1951, but they all died before they could be placed aboard the awaiting ship.

During 1955 and 1956 other attempts were made to translocate sea otters, but in each instance, Kenyon later noted, the animals' fur had become so soiled that when they were put in water again, there appeared to be no hope for their survival. In 1959, with previous lessons taken into account and with speedy transplant made possible by the use of an airplane, partial success resulted when otters were released at St. Paul Island (one of the two main Pribilof Islands). They survived for some time, but not long enough to mature, reproduce and establish a new colony.

Translocations carried out from Alaska in the 1960s and 1970s eventually showed that the procedure can be successful. The immediate survival rate is low, however, and small groups of sea otters frequently can't survive long enough to reproduce and establish a permanent colony. Shortly after arrival in a new area, several otters will usually strike out on their own to an uncertain fate.

Jameson, who has monitored a number of the more recent translocations, said that one of the early lessons learned was that sea otters "needed a holding area where they could groom themselves. If the pelage is soiled or dirty, it no longer keeps the water from their skin. If they were soiled during the trip, when they were forced into the water, they died."

He said a translocation made in 1970 to one Washington State site provided "a better habitat and a better survival rate. They (sea otters) had holding pens, they were fed for a couple days, they were cleaned and acclimated before they were released. We've seen growth every year we've been up there. In 1983 we saw 52."

Summing up the result of several years of translocating sea otters, Jameson told me, "We just resurveyed the Alaska population and that certainly has been a successful translocation in southeast Alaska. It appears it may be successful in British Columbia. We are optimistic in Washington; it looks like it is going to take off. Oregon was a failure."

According to Carl Benz, the Fish and Wildlife coordinator for the Sea Otter Recovery Program, three sites are considered possible for translocation to enlarge the southern sea otter population: San Nicolas Island, the Northern California coast, or off southern Oregon.

San Nicolas has always been considered because its waters are rich in nutrients, making it ideal for both otter and shellfish, and because it is out of direct shipping lanes where accidental oil spills could contaminate the habitat.

Ebert, however, feels that San Nicolas Island is a bad choice because some mariculture leases have already been let there. He adds, "From our Department's studies, there's no possibility that the sea otters would (all) stay at San Nicolas. The distance between islands there is not all that great. They are a mobile population; you'll always find an otter or two or three who will range very widely. If there are too many males, the female leaves the area. In the mating process the male grabs the nose of the female and he can rip it off. The female leaves for her own safety!"

Jameson, of Fish and Wildlife, feels the majority of the sea otter population would remain. "I believe it's over 20 miles to the nearest island," he commented, "and about 60 to the mainland."

The debate over the feasibility of translocation as a means of expanding the California population—as well as the desirability of expanding that population—will probably continue to be argued even as it is being carried out.

*Following page: Sharp teeth are handy for getting out that last morsel of crab.* ▶

*A banged-up nose, like this female's at right, means that she has mated.*

*Mother and baby enjoy eating out.*

*Mother otter shares lunch with her pup.*

# A Sea Otter Forest

*The number of living creatures of all Orders, whose existence intimately depends on the kelp, is wonderful. A great volume might be written, describing the inhabitants of one of these beds of seawood . . . I can only compare these great aquatic forests . . . with the terrestrial ones in the intertropical regions. Yet, if in any country a forest was destroyed, I do not believe nearly so many species of animals would perish as would here, from the destruction of the kelp.*

This observation by Charles Darwin, written in 1834 during the *Beagle's* visit to Chile, is used to open a significant article by Ronald H. McPeak and Dale A. Glantz on the use of California's kelp beds, which was published in the Spring 1984 issue of *Oceanus* magazine. McPeak is the senior marine biologist at Kelco, which manufactures a variety of alginates derived from the kelp scientifically identified as *Macrocystis pyrifera*. Glantz is also a member of the staff.

This kelp, which grows in vast underwater forests off the California coast, provides alginates used to help stabilize, thicken, suspend and gel a number of food products and pharmaceuticals. They find their way into our lives in products such as ice cream, beer, TV dinners, juice drinks, salad dressings, toothpaste, pet foods, milkshakes, baked goods and dressings. Alginates are also used in industrial applications such as textile print pastes and paper coatings.

Sea otters act as aquatic forest rangers in the beds of kelp, great and small, that are their home. They live amidst the kelp, rest atop the kelp, give birth to their babies on a bed of kelp, and most important, feed on sea urchins, which can destroy a kelp forest like a swarm of locusts can ravage a field of grain.

This means that the sea otter also preys on clams and abalone in these areas, making themselves unpopular with the shellfish business. At the same time, by consuming large quantities of sea urchins, they contribute to the multimillion-dollar kelp industry. Red sea urchins, which are exported to Asia, are harvested for considerable profit, but on a smaller scale. The figures indicate that the greater contribution to the American economy is made through the processing of kelp.

In a personal communication, VanBlaricom expanded on this subject:

*It is suggested frequently that urchin fishermen are taking the place of sea otters as "rangers" of the kelp forest in southern California, where the sea otters do not occur. I regard this view as incorrect, for several reasons. First, two species of sea urchins (red and purple) occur in the kelp forests of California when sea otters are absent. The fishery takes only red urchins. Purple urchins can be quite abundant, are known to be capable of destructive overgrazing of kelp populations, and may increase in numbers as a result of the fishery if competition with red urchins is important (there is evidence that it is). Second, effort by urchin fishermen varies significantly with quality of urchin roe (the egg masses and associated tissues are considered delicacies in Asian markets), weather and sea conditions, and especially as a result of changing market conditions such as price structure, demand, and competition from fisheries in the other parts of the world. As a result, fishing activity can vary greatly over time. Thus, urchin fishermen are far less effective as "rangers" than sea otters.*

Both the California Department of Fish & Game and

the U.S. Fish and Wildlife Service have studied the kelp, sea urchins and the impact of the sea otters on both for a number of years. In 1973, more than 10 years before Van-Blaricom offered his conclusions, the Department of Fish & Game published "Fish Bulletin 158," written by department researchers Daniel J. Miller and John J. Geibel. They came to some conclusions that have been confirmed in later studies by others:

*Kelp canopies are important as protective cover for fish and sea otters, as substrate or food for small organisms that may be eaten by larger kelp bed residents, and the canopy supplies food to benthic herbivores when deteriorated fronds or broken blades settle to the bottom.*

*In central California a major realignment of benthic invertebrate distribution and biomass in kelp beds has resulted from the foraging habits of the sea otter,* Enhydra lutris . . . *Minter (1971), in his kelp bed study near Monterey, stated: "Though no observations were made during this study of what otters are eating in the Del Monte kelp beds, divers found ample evidence to indicate that a once extensive abalone population had been annihilated. Numerous shells of the Red Abalone* (Haliotis rufescens) *were observed littering the bottom, yet not a single living animal was seen. In addition, no living specimens of the red urchin,* Strongylocentrotus franciscanus, *and a very few of the smaller purple urchin,* S. purpuratus, *were observed."*

*It has been established that urchin removal results in increased vegetative growth . . . however, the increase in* Macrocystis *observed by North (1965) in central California occurred outside of as well as within the established foraging range of sea otters . . . The zones where sea otter predation may have contributed to*

*increased* Macrocystis *densities were from Pt. Pinos to Lover's Pt. (the Monterey Peninsula) and near San Simeon; however, no data were collected in these zones to assign the degree of kelp enhancement to sea otter predation or to favorable environmental conditions.*

Ten years later VanBlaricom completed his exhaustive study of the effect of sea otters on kelp beds as part of his work for the U.S. Fish and Wildlife Service and it has been reviewed, approved and published. His findings establish that the presence of sea otters has a major favorable effect on the kelp beds and has a direct contribution to the enhancement of the kelp harvest. He wrote in part:

*The composition of kelp assemblages has also changed in areas reoccupied by sea otters, shifting toward dominance by the kelp species most desired by kelp harvesting interests. Such patterns have emerged in a number of locations in California in association with expansion of the range of the sea otters. I briefly review published information on the relationship of kelp bed enhancement to stock sizes of associated finfish populations and suggest that sea otters can also cause enlargement of fish stocks available for commercial and recreational utilization.*

At the start of his paper, VanBlaricom states: "My principal goal here is to present evidence that sea otters have significant positive effects on harvestable kelp resources in central California, and as a consequence, have positive effects on fish populations that associate with kelp forests."

In his discussion of the interaction of sea otters and kelp in Alaska and Canada, he writes:

*In Alaska and Canada, studies of the effects of sea otters on kelp forest structure have produced consistent results. Separate studies in the Aleutian Islands, southeastern Alaska, and Vancouver Island all have shown that sea otters control the abundance of sea urchins, which are otherwise capable of grazing kelp populations to the point of virtual extinction. The removal of sea urchins by sea otters fosters the proliferation of kelps and profoundly alters the composition and dynamics of the kelp forest ecosystem . . . In the Aleutian archipelago, enhancement of kelp beds by sea otters produces substantial enlargement of fish stocks that associate with kelps. In turn, larger fish stocks seem to attract increased number of fish-eating birds and mammals.*

As for the kelp in the sea otters' southern range, VanBlaricom writes: "There are many similarities between kelp forest ecosystems in Alaska and California. In both regions, kelps are the predominant sources of plant biomass produced near shore, and kelp populations are important structural and trophic components in the habitats of many species of finfish and shellfish . . . Sea urchins are the principal grazers of large algae in both locations, and sea otters are the most efficient consumers of sea urchins and many other herbivorous macroinvertebrates."

VanBlaricom states that in southern California, where there are no sea otters, kelp harvesting firms have to devote considerable effort and money to control or eliminate sea urchins from the kelp beds, which they lease from the state. Harvesting off central California, however, has increased in recent years. When populations of important natural urchin predators—sea otters, lobsters, fishes—are reduced or eliminated by human activity, the task and the cost of control of sea urchin necessarily falls to the kelp harvesters.

He notes that the kelp forests have increased significantly in areas where the sea otters have returned, such as the regions near Carmel Bay and Point Lobos and in sectors along the Big Sur coast. "During the summer of 1975 beds of *Nereocystis* were larger and denser than at any time prior to the return of the sea otters to the area." (McPeak, in a personal communication to me, feels the difference was even more dramatic in 1978.) "By August of 1982 *Macrocystis* was the predominant canopy species . . . Should this trend continue without interruption from winter weather of unusual severity, the kelp canopies of the area will likely become large and dense enough to support kelp harvesting activities."

VanBlaricom touched on a topic that became something of a household word during the winter of 1982–83: El Niño. One effect of this natural phenomenon is the unnatural warming of waters far north of the equator, bringing fish and bird populations usually found in waters much warmer than normal off California. Because of the changing ocean surface temperatures, El Niño is also responsible for howling wind storms at sea. Swells build up that can devastate entire forests of kelp. This happened during 1982–83's El Niño, setting back the progress made in the enlargement of the kelp range.

(While early 1983 popularized El Niño in common knowledge, it was not the first year that the West Coast had experienced the climatic deviation. A strong El Niño occurred in the winter of 1955–56, again in the late fifties, and in 1972–73. Weaker ones, with only minimal effects, took place in the early months of other years, including 1951, 1963 and 1975.)

VanBlaricom concludes his paper with an observation on kelp and fish: "The importance of kelp forest habitat for maintenance of fish stocks of value to ocean fishermen has been widely recognized in California. Kelp forests foster increased sizes of associated finfish populations by increasing substrate area, increasing the amount of shelter for juvenile fishes seeking refuge from predators, and by enlarging the habitats and food bases of surface-associated organisms on which fish forage."

He also pointed out that the sea otter's ultimate role is decidedly a beneficial one for humans: "While shellfish populations can be reduced significantly within months of the arrival of sea otters, the expansion of harvestable kelp resources may not occur for a decade or more. As a result, management interest understandably focuses on the highly visible initial effects of the sea otters."

In an article in *Oceanus*, McPeak and Glantz explain the importance of kelp:

*The marine forests of California not only create a unique eco-system for a myriad of animals, but also benefit man in a variety of ways. Giant kelp contains iodine, potassium, and other minerals, vitamins and carbohydrates, and has been used for years as a food supplement. Of more value, however, kelp is the principal source of algin, a natural substance obtained from the processing of kelp, with the special ability to control large quantities of water.*

*Giant kelp has no root structure as found in land plants. Instead, kelp has a complex of branching, pencil-sized strands, called a holdfast, that clings to the ocean floor. Fronds originate at*

*the base of the plant, near the holdfast, and eventually grow to the surface. The fronds are composed of a stemlike stipe and numerous blades that attach to the stipe by a short pedicel. At the base of the blades, gas-filled bladders serve to float the fronds away from the bottom. While land vegetation takes most of its nourishment through its roots, giant kelp absorbs nutrients from the water through all its surfaces. Mature kelp plants form a thick "canopy" of fronds on the surface. Under optimal conditions, when nutrient levels are high and ocean temperatures are low, fronds can elongate at phenomenal rates. Researchers at Scripps Institution of Ocean-ography (at La Jolla, California) have measured Macrocystis fronds elongating at 60 centimeters (2 feet) a day.*

McPeak and Glantz describe the danger sea urchins pose to the kelp forests:

*A variety of animals, including the sea urchin, can also affect the abundance and distribution of kelp. Under normal conditions, sea urchins feed upon drift algae, which becomes available through natural processes of kelp dislodgement and degradation. Giant kelp of all stages is grazed and destroyed when urchins become over-populated or when there is a reduction in the availability of drift material. David Leighton and Wheeler J. North, both formerly at Scripps, documented massive migrations of sea urchins off the coast of San Diego in the early 1960s. Leighton recorded the destruction of 1.6 hectares of Macrocystis during a two-month period as urchins moved through the forest at a rate of 10 meters a month.*

McPeak and Glantz then enlarge upon what we have already learned about the uses of kelp. Kelco, founded in

1929, continues to maintain several processing locations and research laboratories in San Diego.

"Initially, Kelco produced kelp meal, a milled, dried form of *Macrocystis*, for livestock feed. Soon thereafter, Kelco began to extract algin from freshly harvested kelp. The fresh kelp was unloaded, chopped, cooked, and further processed to yield this unique compound, algin, first used to control the viscosity in a gasket compound for sealing tin cans. Through continued research, Kelco developed many applications for algin. The company presently manufactures about 70 different algin products for literally hundreds of different uses."

McPeak and Glantz explain that initially men harvested the kelp from a barge, using long poles.

*Present day harvesters also cut* Macrocystis *canopies with reciprocating blades mounted at the base of a conveyor system. Modern harvesters have the conveyor system (drapers) mounted on the stern of the vessel. When the harvester arrives at the kelp bed, drapers are lowered into the water to a depth of 0.9 meters, main engines are secured, and a bow propellor pushes the vessel stern-first through the water. These harvesters operate like seagoing lawnmowers, pushing the large cutting racks through the kelp bed, gathering the cut kelp on conveyors that carry the kelp aboard and deposit it into a bin. Modern harvesters carry as much as 550 metric tons of* Macrocystis, *which can be collected during a day of harvesting. The kelp industry in California has harvested as much as 156,000 metric tons in a single year.*

The State of California regulates the harvesting of kelp to maintain healthy beds; kelp may be cut no deeper than four feet below the water's surface. The beds are leased from the state for 20-year periods and the fee is paid depending on how many tons are harvested. A few areas are designated "open" by the state and any company may harvest there after obtaining a permit.

In the kelp forests too far south to benefit from the services of the sea otter "rangers," Kelco has as many as 15 divers on its payroll to control the grazing of purple and white sea urchins in some southern California lease areas!

*Sometimes, life is just a big yawn.*

*A resting sea otter peaks over some kelp.*

◄ *This page and previous page: One otter has been caught, tagged with color-coded plastic, and released so the Fish & Game Department can study its movement patterns.*

# Where to See Them

There are sea otters among us and we can go see them. They can be viewed in the wild, though not on command. For those of us who cannot reach them in their preferred, and often quite isolated, habitats, great difficulties have been overcome in the preparation of man-made facilities where sea otters can reside. The knowledge gained by keeping a few captive otters has been applied to enhancing their chances of survival in the wild.

Young people, especially, should meet *Enhydra lutris* as early in life as possible, and the seaquariums and aquariums offer a stimulating educational experience in this respect. At the present time there are five places where the public can view sea otters: Sea World in San Diego; the Vancouver Public Aquarium in British Columbia; the Seattle Aquarium and the Point Defiance Zoo and Aquarium in Tacoma, both in Washington State; and the newest of all, the Monterey Bay Aquarium on Monterey 's Cannery Row.

I opt to watch them in nature when I can. This book has already made the joys of Point Lobos State Reserve abundantly clear. It is a four-mile drive south of Carmel and is the Pacific Coast's gem in the world of nature. In winter months, the otters tend to remain in the shelter of Whalers Cove and the nameless cove five minutes' walk to the north, off Moss Beach. In calmer months, they may be seen less frequently in the sheltered parts, and more often in the relatively open waters, on either side of Punta de los Lobos Marinos. This is the actual tip of the Reserve which points to the rocky islands where the sea lions live. Vantage points are reached within two or three minutes' walk from the Headland Trail parking lot. The otters are often seen within Headland Cove itself and off the promontory overlooking Sandhill Cove. Within five minutes I have counted a dozen in each location! Isolated otters are often spotted all along the Reserve's shoreline; at the southern boundary off Bird Rock, toward Gibson Beach, a raft is again often seen.

At Monterey itself, besides at the marina and within the harbor, sea otters are often seen all along Cannery Row, but it is often difficult to get a clear view because of the buildings. A couple of the restaurants on the shoreline itself offer fine viewing.

Ten miles south of Carmel is Garrapata State Beach. A hike across the field and down to the beach itself is often rewarded with sightings of sea otters. Less than 10 miles further south is Andrew Molera State Park, and isolated sightings of sea otters have been made from atop its cliffs.

Sightings of sea otters during the rest of the drive down the Big Sur Coast are unpredictable. The best thing to do is to look for the bobbing brown masses of seaweed, then take a detailed look with binoculars. There you may see a sea otter strapped into this sea cradle.

San Luis Obispo County can be entered from the north either by the coastal route through Big Sur or from inland. On the inland approach, via Highway 101, watch for Route 46 (west) about 20 miles before reaching the San Luis Obispo area. This is the cutoff through the hills to San Simeon and Hearst Castle. The William Randolph Hearst Memorial State Beach is at San Simeon; from the pier, you can sometimes glimpse the otters. All along this coast— from Piedras Blancas Lighthouse, south past the Hearst Beach and Cayucos, Morro Strand and Atascadero State Beaches—the sea otter has started to expand the southern reaches of his range. South of Morro Bay, seven miles south of Los Osos, is Montana de Oro State Park, which also has vantage points over sea otter waters.

This, then, is the heart of California's sea otter country: from Santa Cruz east and south to Moss Landing, where they have recently taken up residence, on south along the Monterey Peninsula and through Big Sur, and finally the San Luis Obispo County coast to Pismo Beach and Montana de Oro.

"It's strange," Fish and Wildlife biologist Ron Jameson told me, "but Morro Bay has been the heart of the area where there has been controversy over sea otters ravaging the abalone and Pismo clam population . . . but now people swarm all over the place just to get a glimpse of the sea otters! Sea-otter watching is a popular pastime."

I have been paying periodic visits to the Monterey marina to keep tabs on a total of five sea otters. Two are mothers, one with a very young baby who screams to high heaven every time his mother leaves him to look for lunch. Usually the baby is atop the mother, snoozing, being groomed or feeding on his mother's milk. In this position, the baby sea otter looks like a furry growth with neither face nor limbs. On rare occasions, he will float on his back at a slight angle from his mother; then it is apparent that he is a fine young otter in his own right!

The other mother's baby is three or four months old. The older offspring no longer wails at brief separations as the baby does; once the mother surfaces, she breaks open the clam shell and shares the food with the youngster every time. Some biologists believe a mother and youngster will remain together for almost a year; most agree there is no more solicitous mother in nature than the sea otter. Mother and baby are rarely apart, except for food-gathering, until the juvenile is at least seven or eight months old.

The fifth sea otter is something of a disgrace. He begs for a living—we would like to think a sea otter had more class than to carry out such an activity! He has discovered the easy life at the end of Fisherman's Wharf, where sport fishing and party boats come in to tie up. The fishermen dump fish heads and entrails overboard as they approach the dock. Over the years a constant screaming canopy of gulls greets the boats' arrival and at wharfside a resident population of sea lions begs shamelessly for food. This one unfortunate sea otter has joined this band.

Compounding this, small trays of fish are sold on the wharf to tourists as "sea lion food." Humans who enjoy making nature sit up and beg buy this leftover bait to feed to the wildlife. The Department of Fish & Game points out that this practise makes marine mammals, gulls and pelicans so tame that they become easy prey to human meanness. Some commercial fishermen consider the sea lion a voracious competitor; sea lions dead with bullet wounds continue to pop up on California's beaches and a number of pelicans have had their pouches and beaks slashed.

Monterey 's marina has had resident sea otters since the late 1960s. One, named Oscar until she disappeared for a few months and returned with a baby, was renamed Oscarina. In 1979 or 1980 her carcass was found near Moss Landing, on the other side of the bay from Monterey. She may have succumbed to old age.

The Seattle Aquarium is located at the city 's Waterfront Park and has had otters since 1977. At the time of this writing there are six. The original otters were captured in Prince William Sound, Alaska, in 1976 and 1977. Seattle's original sea otter, Tak, died in 1983 of growths in his liver and spleen. He lived to his normal life expectancy and sired four otters at the Aquarium. (Sea otter science is not complete. Some biologists say that sea otters can live in nature to 30 years of age. Most agree that the normal lifespan is 15 to 20 years.)

The Point Defiance Zoo and Aquarium at Tacoma, Washington, has had otters since 1969. They now have four, one male and three females. Two earlier sea otters died; one was a male "who died of old age" at more than 10 years of age. The female died "of stress-related problems" at the age of 14 or 15. The present quartet was captured near Cordova, Alaska.

San Diego's Sea World has had otters since December 1972. Spokeswoman Jackie O'Connor told me that "although several have been born here at Sea World, we have not had a long-surviving pup to date. The otters were originally from the Monterey Bay area and are here under the auspices of the California Department of Fish & Game. Among the work that is being conducted with them is a study to help understand their daily nutritional needs."

The Vancouver Aquarium, according to Stefani Hewlett, the Aquarium biologist, received its first sea otter in 1969, a three-year-old male on breeding loan from Point Defiance. He lived at the Aquarium alone for the next three years. Two females were received in July 1972 as part of a joint Canadian–United States transplant operation on the west coast of Vancouver Island.

The original male is still there, in retirement in a reserve pool. His age is estimated at 18 years. The females have since given birth and Vancouver's sea otter colony has beguiled such visitors as Queen Elizabeth II. One baby otter died at the age of eight months "as the result of an unfortunate accident," Mrs. Hewlett stated. The baby 's natural curiosity caused it to become trapped under a pool grate, where it drowned.

Asked to comment on the problems of keeping sea otters in captivity, Mrs. Hewlett drew on her considerable experience to point out a number of things the general public often takes for granted. "Regarding the difficulties of rearing youngsters in captivity, there is really no problem if they are reared by their parents, or rather, their mothers.

"There is the usual problem in any young mammal, in that they are highly exploratory and can create problems for themselves, (such as this particular juvenile lifting the grate). However, rearing an infant that has been orphaned is an entirely different matter and in most cases involves two great challenges: 1) trying to replace the mother as a source of food, grooming, security and teacher; 2) typically an orphan is debilitated anyway and starts out at reduced body weight and a high stress load as a result of not having any parent.

"Orphans in the wild are a natural phenomenon and all would die in any case, so that lack of success by an aquarium or other support facility is incorrectly viewed as failure; it is more properly an attempt to overcome nearly insurmountable odds.

"Loss of older juveniles in the wild as a result of an adventuresome spirit is also not unusual. They may stray too far from their mothers, get caught and drown in crab traps, eat something inappropriate or become some other animal's lunch. Nature takes care of these losses by over-production of young."

Mrs. Hewlett's comments are echoed by Dr. Thomas D. Williams, a Monterey veterinarian whose responsibilities include care of the new Monterey Bay Aquarium's otters. Because there is a fair population of sea otters in the Monterey area, he has spent a number of years caring for orphans. He says the facilities at the Aquarium not only permit the objectives of education and public display but also offer vastly improved means for research.

The object of sea otter research "is to improve the outlook of the population as a whole." He points out the difference between caring for a wild orphaned animal and ministering to a household pet. The pet can almost be likened to a human patient, whose medical and family history are known. With the wild sea otter, the odds of success are not encouraging.

"In wild animals," he stated, "you do not have a history of the individual animal and this makes medical treatment more difficult. Part of our studies at the Aquarium will be to investigate normal physiology and behavior in sea otters.

"You're dealing with an orphan animal and it is going to die unless you intervene. We have to learn their reaction to stress, not just disease. There are so many things we don't know about sea otters."

Dr. Williams says a considerable body of knowledge has been acquired over recent years from orphans taken to the SPCA or his office, even from those that did not survive. Also, surgical techniques have been developed. He recalled a recent instance in Monterey where a sea otter was found suffering from a twisted intestine; surgery corrected the problem and the animal was released back to the wild.

Work is also now progressing on how to de-oil sea otters. This, of course, is a great concern in California waters, where a major oil spill could be catastrophic. Now that a government grant has been awarded to study the effects of oil on the pelage, animals caught in a spill may be saved, he says. "We've analyzed the chemical and physical makeup of the fur. The rest is in the experimental stage." (Any attempt at saving otters hit by oil, of course, would then depend on how fast human intervention could be brought about.)

Dr. Williams and Pat Quinn of the Monterey Bay Aquarium staff are preparing a paper on the care and feeding of orphaned sea otters. The rough draft of this paper reveals some fascinating tidbits. A sea otter is generally four pounds at birth. Sea otter pups feed every two hours and start off eating about a pound of food a day; high fat and low apparent lactose are hallmarks of marine mammal milk. A substitute diet used successfully on orphaned pups included fine ground clams, water, 5 percent dextrose, fish oil, calcium, Hivite vitamins and Diaglow. After one month, the sea otter pups were fed clams, abalone, sea urchins, mussels, black cod and squid.

The young sea otters were kept on a water bed, which gave the feel and surge of water. Dr. Williams and Pat Quinn found that the juvenile otters became bored easily. To remedy this, they were given plastic baby toys to keep them diverted.

One recent orphan, Dr. Williams wrote, was "constantly held, groomed, petted and played with, unless he slept. For all points and purposes he was treated like a human baby, which we feel was necessary for his survival." A mother otter spends a great deal of time grooming the young one. "Seventy-five percent of a pup's life is spent out of the water while resting on the female's chest." As Dr. Williams discovered, baby sea otters are not much different from other babies except, perhaps, that they demand more maternal attention.

Sea otters evoke the same response from people that babies do, or teddy bears, or koalas. Those whose interests conflict with the sea otter's needs admit they have a hard time talking against this creature. If this modest book has one overriding message, it is that there must be room for both. It is to the everlasting shame of the human race that any natural resource has been so depleted that it cannot flourish unhindered and must instead be "managed."

*This mother sea otter decided it was time for a baby photo.*

*This sea otter pup is waiting for its mother to return from a foraging dive.*

*A baby sea otter takes a relaxing siesta on her mother's stomach.*

*Mother keeps a wary eye out while junior takes a nap.*

*Following page: Mother becomes a floating home for this pup as it emerges from the water and shakes its fur.* ▶

*Page 87: A mother otter holds her napping pup.*

*Mother and baby have matching mustaches!*

*Epilogue: A Second Chance?*

*Margaret Owings*
*Founder and President*
*Friends of the Sea Otter*

Low tide—and the sea lies like pewter with a polish of silver from the slant of the morning sun. Heavy brine, that life-giving support, slides out and slips back under the massive canopy of kelp with a momentum that rolls pebbles onto intimate beaches and draws them back to the underwater world.

But now one perceives another subtlety through the magnified clarity of the water—the flowing grace in motion of a California sea otter, exploring with its forepaws and navigating with its webbed hind feet. Another otter bursts through the pattern of kelp, whiskers fanning out like the struts of a parasol as it parts the fronds, holding between its paws a clutch of mussels ripped from the nearshore rocks below the surface.

The privilege of watching this smallest of marine mammals from the shore offers each of us a personal reunion with life in the sea. Coastal residents who venture out to experience the grandeur of a storm may spot what appears to be a small dark log, sliding down a wave, tossed and spun, inundated and swept into apparent oblivion. After that momentary glimpse, the sea otter simply vanishes.

Gradually, as we familiarize ourselves with the little otter, the whole ecology of the coast commences to unfold. An empathy is exchanged between us as the sea otter plays and splashes, tipping and floating, alertly raising its head to focus upon us with curiosity before it turns with a flip and somersaults below the surface. This vitality draws people to the edge of the sea, its sands, its promontories as well as to the underwater world in which the otter pursues a key role. "The sense of continuing creation," remarked Rachel Carson. "The relentless drive of life!"

We are struck by the helpless innocence of this animal—and also its undeniable strength, its valiant return from near extinction. Following the holocaust of the fur trade, when herds were scattered and slaughtered, the once unlimited freedom of these playful animals in the lap and slap of the sea appeared nearly gone. But a few clung to survival below the rugged Big Sur cliffs. The otter was to be given a second chance.

Today, however, this remnant population must seek its existence in an overstrained marine environment—overstrained not by otters but by increasing and cumulative human pressures.

How can we ensure the California sea otter a continuity of life? Will it always be menaced by man? How can we protect it from offshore oil spills? Must it be a vassal to man, with man's management and man's manipulations limiting its freedom?

These are questions that sparked the initiative in 1968 to found Friends of the Sea Otter, with its dictate to stand firmly behind a sound conservation program for this unique sea mammal. As the meaning of their rarity became clearer, the public's response was awakened.

Threats and jeopardies to the sea otter's welfare became more exposed. The abalone fishermen did not regard the sea otter as a "rarity back from extinction" but as a predator in competition with man. Yet the immense shell mounds piled like dikes along the shore lands told their own silent story of man's relation to these shellfish—one of excessive exploitation. Actions by the abalone industry as well as violations of the otter's protected status reinforced the realization that this little mammal truly needed a friend.

Is there no room for the sea otter? The food items upon which it relies for its very existence are becoming exhausted by the burgeoning human population. Why shouldn't man share the coastal marine resources with other mammals who can't fill their market baskets at the grocery store? For we are allies, sharing a world with narrowing boundaries.

In the confines of a rich pattern of kelp, a mother otter emerges through the strands and moves directly to her screaming pup. She rolls her body to lie on her back, lifting this eager clinging baby to her chest where she grooms and blows her breath under the surface of its wet fur, causing it to stand up like thistledown. Then, reversing the position of the tiny body, she places her baby 's head on her nipples. In the gentle rocking cradle of the sea, the mother stretches her neck and head in contentment, her forepaws held high.

These rafting otters are tragically susceptible to an oil spill. Oil terminal activities at both ends of the otter range and the encroachment of lease sales for offshore oil drilling pose a permanent threat to the entire sea otter population along the California coast. The greatest likelihood of an oil spill is during the winter months, with oil drift reaching otters drawn together into large rafts in the remaining storm-torn kelp beds.

Once sacrificed in man's frantic rush for fur, then unjustly attacked by man's unwillingness to share the shellfish and now facing a far-reaching jeopardy to its life and habitat by man's reckless drive for oil.

Is this the sea otter's second chance?

◄ *Previous page: An unused rope-boat mooring substitutes for a kelp bed in Monterey Harbor.*

*After a successful dive, both otter and human surface for a breath of fresh air.*

*A skin diver loses his raft to a visiting sea otter.*

# Glossary

While I have written in strictly conventional English, some of those I have quoted have not. This is a very brief list of the words that sent me to the dictionary the first time I found them used in terms of marine biology.

**Benthic.** Of, or pertaining to, or living on the bottom of or at the greatest depths of a large body of water

**Biomass.** The management of a species population per unit of area

**Clinal.** A graded series of differences

**Cohort.** Belonging to the same generation or age group

**Crustacea.** A class of arthropod animals having jointed feet and mandibles, two pairs of antennae and segmented, chitin-encased bodies, such as lobsters and crabs

**Degradation.** Wearing down, eroding, reduction

**Demography.** Population study

**Depredation.** *See* Predation

**Echinodermata.** A phylum of exclusively marine animals distinguished from all others by an internal skeleton composed of calcite plates and a water-vascular system to serve the needs of locomotion, respiration, nutrition or perception (as in sea urchins)

**Exploitation.** Use

**Extirpate.** To uproot, destroy, make extinct

**Herbivores.** Mammals that feed on plant life

**Infaunal.** Living in the bottom sediment of a body of water

**Intertidal** (zone). The part of the littoral zone above low-tide mark

**Invertebrate.** Animals that lack a spinal column and internal skeleton (in this case, as opposed to finfish)

**Littoral** (zone). Of or pertaining to the zone between the high- and low-water marks

**Molluscs.** Snails, slugs, octopuses, squids, clams, mussels, oysters

**Mortality.** Death rate

**Pelage.** The coat of an animal, fur, or hair

**Pelagic.** Pertaining to the open sea

**Perturbation.** Any effect that makes a small modification in a physical system

**Predation.** The killing and eating of an individual of one species by an individual of another species

**Raft.** The term used to describe a group of sea otters gathered together in a permanent or temporary unit

**Recruitment.** Replenish by reproduction

**Substrate.** Underlayer, the base upon which an organism grows

**Tactile.** Sense of touch

**Taxonomy.** A study aimed at producing a hierarchical system of classification of organisms that best reflects the totality of similarities and differences

**Test.** A hard external covering or shell

**Vibrissae.** Whiskers

# Bibliography

Ames, Jack A., and Morejohn, G. Victor. *Evidence of White Shark, Carcharodon Carcharias, Attacks on Sea Otters, Enhydra Lutris.* Sacramento: California Department of Fish & Game, 1980.

Bancroft, Hubert Howe. *The Works of—History of Alaska.* San Francisco: A. L. Bancroft, 1886.

Boucher, V. J. *Backtracking the Sea Otter.* (Reprint from *Alaska Sportsman.*) Chicago: J. G. Ferguson Publishing, 1960.

Chapman, Joseph A., and Feldhamer, George A., eds. *Wild Mammals of North America.* Baltimore and London: Johns Hopkins University Press, 1982.

Chevigny, Hector. *Lord of Alaska.* New York: Viking Press, 1943.

Grinnell, Joseph; Dixon, Joseph S.; and Linsdale, Jean M. *Fur-Bearing Mammals of California.* Berkeley: University of California Press, 1937.

Henning, Robert A., chief ed. *Islands of the Seals.* Vol. 9, no. 3; Anchorage: The Alaska Geographic Society, 1982.

Hines, Anson H., and Pearse, John S. "Abalones, Shells, and Sea Otters: Dynamics of Prey Populations in Central California." *Ecology 63,* no. 5. Durham, N.C.: Duke University Press, 1982.

Jameson, Ronald J.; Kenyon, Karl W.; Johnson, Ancel M.; and Wight, Howard M. *History and Status of Translocated Sea Otter Populations in North America.* Wildlife Society Bulletin 10 (1982) 100–107.

Jameson, Ronald J. *Evidence of Birth of a Sea Otter on Land in Central California.* California Department of Fish & Game 69 (1983) 122–123.

Kenyon, Karl W. *The Sea Otter in the Eastern Pacific Ocean.* Washington, D.C.: U.S. Government Printing Office, 1969.

Leatherwood, Stephen; Harronton-Coulombe, Linda J.; and Hubbs, Carl L. *Relict Survival of the Sea Otter in Central California and Evidence of its Recent Redispersal South of Point Conception.* Bulletin of Southern California Academy of Sciences 77 (1978).

Lister-Kaye, John. *The White Island.* New York: Dutton, 1973.

Maxwell, Gavin. *Ring of Bright Water.* New York: Dutton, 1961.

McPeak, Ron H., and Glantz, Dale A. "Harvesting California's Kelp Forests." *Oceanus,* Spring, 1984.

Miller, Daniel J., and Geibel, John J. *Summary of Blue Rockfish and Lingcod Life Histories; A Reef Ecology Study; and Giant Kelp, Macrocystis Pyrifera, Experiments in Monterey Bay, California.* Sacramento: California Department of Fish & Game, 1973.

Ogden, Adele. *The California Sea Otter Trade: 1784–1848.* Berkeley and Los Angeles: University of California Press, 1941.

Ogden, Adele. "Russian Sea-Otter and Seal Hunting on the California Coast 1803–1841." *Quarterly of the California Historical Society* 12 (1933), no. 3.

Rearden, Jim, chief ed. *Alaska Mammals.* Vol. 8, no. 2. Anchorage: Alaska Geographic Society, 1981.

# Acknowledgments

Scammon, Charles M. *The Marine Mammals of the Northwestern Coast of North America.* New York: Dover Publications, 1968.

Scheffer, Victor B. *The Amazing Sea Otter.* New York: Charles Scribner's Sons, 1981.

Scheffer, Victor B. *A Natural History of Marine Mammals.* New York: Charles Scribner's Sons, 1976.

Seed, Alice. *Sea Otter in Eastern North Pacific Waters.* Seattle: Pacific Search, 1972.

VanBlaricom, Glenn R. "Relationships of Sea Otters to Living Marine Resources in California: A New Perspective." In: Edited by V. Lyle. Proceedings of the Ocean Studies Symposium, vol. 2, Policy papers. Nov., 1982. Sacramento: California Coastal Commission and California Department of Fish & Game, in press.

*Additional illustration credits:*

Right flap, copyright © 1988
Monterey Bay Aquarium

I am indebted to a number of busy scientists and lay personnel who set aside time so I could interview them personally. I am especially grateful to Jack Ames, Earl Ebert, Carol Fulton, Ron Jameson, Glenn VanBlaricom and Dr. Tom Williams, all of whom have read the portions of the manuscript of this book where they are quoted. Others who have been especially helpful by mail or telephone include Ron McPeak, Karl Kenyon, James Hogue, Victor B. Scheffer, Stefani Hewlett, Jackie O'Connor and Steven L. Rebuck. Dr. James Mattison has been most kind in helping me obtain photographs. Margaret Owings graciously wrote the epilogue.

Alaska Northwest Publishing Co., Edmonds, Washington, generously supplied me with materials and permission to quote from them. Dover Publications of New York were helpful in obtaining information about Capt. Scammon's work. Permission to quote from their publications, as acknowledged at the appropriate points in the text, has been granted by the University of California Press, Pacific Search Press, as well as individuals cited who own their own copyrights. Sea World in San Diego, The Vancouver Public Aquarium, the Seattle Aquarium and the Monterey Bay Aquarium have been generous in supplying appropriate publications, background sheets and in answering questions. The personnel of the Harrison Memorial Library, Carmel, ferreted out many obscure books and references for me. Thanks also to Monterey Harbormaster Brooks Bowhay.

# Index